CODEPENDENT DISCIPLESHIP

by Nick Galieti & Jennifer Roach MDiv, MA, LMHC, CDP

Nick Galieti
4031 South 1950 West
West Valley City, UT. 84119

Distributed by Eborn Books

TABLE OF CONTENTS

CHAPTER 6 - CONCLUSION

Endnotes

Jennifer Roach is a mental health and chemical dependency therapist. She graduated from Seattle Pacific University with a B.A. in Psychology and went on to earn a Master of Divinity from The Seattle School for Theology and Psychology. She then earned a Master of Mental Health Counseling from Argosy University. Prior to converting to The Church of Jesus Christ of Latter-day Saints in 2019, she was ordained clergy in the Anglican church. She has also worked in a variety of positions serving vulnerable families and adults. Jennifer lives outside of Seattle, Washington with her husband of twenty-five years. They have a college age son and two dogs who keep them busy.

Nick Galieti is a Broadcast and Events Language Producer and an experienced Latter-day Saint podcast host and producer. His podcast work includes podcasting for FairMormon, Book of Mormon Central, Latter-day Saint Perspectives, The Good Word Podcast, and Latter-day Saint MissionCast. He has written the book *Tree of Sacrament* and was editor and contributor to the volume *Doctrine and Covenants 4: A Life of Study in Discipleship.* Prior to his marriage to his wife, Heidi, and becoming a father to five daughters, Nick served a mission to Baton Rouge, Louisiana.

Nick would like to thank:

Brian Murdock for your professional competence, your continued compassion, and for guiding me to a more meaningful life.

My lovely wife, Heidi, for your eternal love, unending support, and for being patient with my bad grammar.

My children for letting me be your dad. Finishing this book is what I mean by the Law of the Harvest. Plant your seeds, nurture them, and see them grow.

PREFACE

A World of Confusion and Chaos

Many people today express feelings of being overwhelmed or taxed beyond their abilities. A growing voice of discontent and victimization seems to underscore the discourse on social media and reports by news outlets. The intense and sometimes all-consuming demands of modern society include worries of economics, employment, friendships, family relationships and responsibilities, moral responses to injustices, church and community obligations, and even conflicts centered around government and politics. Modern scriptures record a description of this type of society, saying, "And all things shall be in commotion; and surely, men's hearts shall fail them; for fear shall come upon all people."[1]

This scripture describes an emotional or mental health pandemic in these last days. For years many have felt the symptoms but didn't know how to diagnose what those symptoms indicated. We have also come to find ways that this "disease" has uniquely impacted members of The Church of

Jesus Christ of Latter-day Saints. Now we can say that we have received further light and knowledge that illuminates the path forward.

Some have viewed being a faithful member of the Church as providing some sort of shield or protection from mental health issues. We hope to stand as a witness that such a notion is not only unfounded but also unnecessary. The presence of mental health issues is neither evidence of nor the consequence of sin. There are many reasons that we experience challenges of all types in this fallen world. At times, the ways in which we interpret the words of scripture and of living prophets can contribute to mental health issues, even when our motivations appear pure. One such scenario arises with respect to the topic of codependency.

Codependency is a matter of mental health. Codependency is typically defined by a distinct set of compulsive behaviors, that includes fixing other people's problems, taking on the burdens of others, or managing the consequences that arise from the actions, misdeeds, tragedies, or trials of others for whom they feel responsible. While there is some ongoing debate regarding a universal definition for codependency, (and as a result there is little to be said of a widely accepted diagnosis), few in the mental health communities would deny its existence. Much has been written and discussed over the past decades on this topic and there is still much to learn. We are venturing into new territory to assert any sort of discourse on the subject of codependency in a spiritual or religious context. Answers to current challenges with devotional burnout, marital stress, and even over zealousness can and should be explored through the lens of codependency.

We, the authors of this text, are deeply connected to codependency. This topic impacts our personal, professional, social, and religious lives in ways that are powerfully informative. It is a burden that we personally carry, but one that has led us to a closer connection with our Savior and his restored gospel. We see others who fight this battle without the knowledge that they are even in a war. We witness the pain it has caused and hope that this text will provide a balm for past wounds and a strengthening agent to meet our exciting and liberating future.

There is a connection between this matter of mental health and the choice of discipleship. Spirituality and mental health intersect, but addressing that topic requires a special delicacy that is not easy to harmonize.

The following quote from a prominent Protestant pastor from the 1920's and 30's, Harry Emerson Fosdick, sums up the challenge that codependency presents in a spiritual context: "Some Christians carry their religion on their backs. It is a packet of beliefs and practices which they must bear. At times it grows heavy and they would willingly lay it down, but that would mean a break with old traditions, so they shoulder it again. But real Christians do not carry their religion, their religion carries them. It is not weight, it is wings. It lifts them up, it sees them over hard places. It makes the universe seem friendly, life purposeful, hope real, sacrifice worthwhile. It sets them free from fear, futility, discouragement, and sin— the great enslaver of men's souls. You can know a real Christian when you see him, by his buoyancy."[2]

All that is experienced in personal, family life, work life—everything can add to an increasingly heavy backpack. Some may wonder why they are experiencing a loss of happiness in spite of all the scriptural and prophetic promises of joy for those who keep the commandments of the Lord. They may even wonder, "Is this a question that has an answer?"

Yes, there is an answer; yes, there is hope.

[*The following is a summarized personal history from Nick Galieti of how he came to develop and experience codependency. While we hope that this story is informative and provides you with some context that may relate to your own personal experiences, you may choose to skip to chapter 1 where we enter the subject matter in greater detail and definition.*]

Nick's Story: Falling into Codependency

Before marriage and after my mission I felt fairly independent in both emotional and temporal matters. I was going to school, had a decent job, a nice apartment, multiple callings in church, life was going well. I felt that I was choosing my path, and I was making steady progress toward the future I envisioned for myself. I was just being me, and I felt I was doing pretty well with that.

After meeting my future wife, Heidi, experiencing courtship, and being married, I still felt some sense of that independence, but with the new dynamic of being a spouse. I was no longer just myself—I was part of a team, an eternal team that wanted the best for the other. No one else in the world was just like our team.

Each relationship takes on a life of its own. For our marriage, I envisioned the symbiotic nature of this new relationship requiring a joint and equal effort by both partners. A relationship where one of the partners feels they are not needed or undervalued will move them to be less concerned with whether that relationship lives or dies. Apathy is relationship cancer—slowly eating away the efficacy of the immune system that enables the relationship to persevere.

After the birth of our first daughter, my wife experienced postpartum depression, and I experienced postpartum neglect. We were no longer the center of each other's universe, and we were no longer in a position to exclusively care for this new relationship we covenanted to maintain. There was competition for our energy, which threw off the balance of our equal partnership in unexpected ways.

Understandably, my wife focused her attention on our newborn child, who literally was dependent on her mother to care for her, nourish her, and keep her alive. Feeling somewhat under qualified to contribute to this parenting endeavor, I turned my attention to our relationship. After all, she was busy dealing with the baby; if I didn't help to maintain our relationship, who would?

I took on the idea that as partners this meant that she would handle the one thing (our child) and I would handle the other things (the house, the money, our relationship, etc.). My contributions to the relationship became temporal in nature. If I provided stuff, then I was doing my part. If she was raising the kid, that was doing her part.

However, my wife and child became the consumers of my "stuff," which made me feel like I was a sort of servant and that I was only valued based on what I provided for them to consume. If I cooked the best food, then I was a good dad. If I provided a nice house, then I was a good dad. If they had movies to watch, video games to play, a yard to play in, then I was a good husband and father. What was worse, this felt like a rational and healthy conclusion in my young mind.

Over time this relationship with my wife became more about stuff than it did about us. Our relationship was more transactional than centered on mutual love and respect. Consequently, we started to drift apart in ways that became painful to both of us—but in different ways. My wife felt she had no way to win: either she neglected the child and became a bad mother in favor of our relationship, or she continued to contribute so little to our marriage relationship that she would feel like a bad wife. She felt like there was a short list of acceptable ways to show love to me. Therefore, if she tried to express her love and care in new ways, they were neither recognized nor accepted.

For me, I felt like I was a bad husband because I was not understanding of her demands and was selfishly needing the attention I was used to getting, and I was a bad father because I felt competitive with our infant, a truly dependent and innocent life.

From 2001 to 2004 we struggled to get started. Southern California, for all its wonderful aspects, was not affordable for young families. After the birth of our second child we decided to move to Utah to find a home where we could raise our family. With a lower cost of living, we fostered a hope that such a scenario would deliver some sense of stability. With stability we could focus on the things that matter most. However, challenges such as ours are not easily solved by geography alone.

Starting in 2004 I went to work hoping to provide for my family's needs in a new part of the country. With a new ward and with new people to meet, I figured that they would be accompanied by new opportunities for friendships. However, postpartum depression would keep rearing its ugly head time and time again because we would keep having children. There was some hope that with each child would come a new life—and new opportunities for happiness. In some ways that was true. However, that is not always a great starting point on the path to happiness.

When we moved to Utah I was working for Guitar Center in the Professional Audio department. I sold microphones, PA systems, mixers— all products I knew about and used as a sound engineer. I loved the products even though the pay was nothing fantastic. An opportunity to become a real estate agent and develop land made its way into my life, dangling a golden carrot in front of this stubborn mule. I chose to leave my safe but meager income at Guitar Center to enter the world of self-employment as a real estate agent. I joined up as a business partner with a former mission companion of mine who was already having enough business that he couldn't handle the load. I viewed this as a good sign. Unlike many who enter self-employment with high risk, I knew I would have a soft landing. Regardless, this was still a very scary step for a young father to make. So, when I quit my job and began with real estate, I certainly didn't expect that business would come to a screeching halt for the next six months. We didn't buy or sell a single house and thus had no income for six months. I wondered what I had done to mess things up that bad.

At this time my wife was becoming more and more distant and less engaged with the world around her. I didn't know what to blame for this change—perhaps not being around family or friends anymore? She knew that was going to happen when we moved, and she agreed to it; so I didn't think there was much I could do. We had a mortgage and this was where we were going to stay. Yet I did promise to love her, and I deeply desired her happiness. I fell back into old patterns. I figured if our home was so amazing, so nice, so well maintained, that she would just overlook the fact that she was so sad. But, with no income, how could I provide anything for her, let alone nice things?

I figured if I were a mess at home, I would need to find something that I could put into the world that would do good. The drive to make order from chaos was growing inside me. There was also a part of me thinking that if I were just more righteous, if I were a better member of the Church, if I went beyond the extra mile, then God would have no choice but to bless me. If I were righteous, He would bless us with a home buyer for our business. If I were doing good in the world, the world would do good to me in return. If I didn't run just the extra mile, but I ran a marathon, I would be blessed with a good job, with a happy wife, or something with which I could find some sense of relief from the sense of failure that was looming all around me. I was so desperate to feel some sense that I wasn't worthless that I volunteered for a two-year service mission for LDS Family Services. As a service missionary I would make videos to help train therapists how to help their clients.

We started to see some increase in our business, but not enough to fully recover from the months of dearth. When the service mission ended in 2007, I was reaching what would be near the bottom of the abyss. My business partner and I were getting desperate to try and find some reason as to why our business was struggling. We tried creative ways to fix the problems, but things were staying broken. I had to start taking work that would help fill in the gaps in between the sparse home sales. But we were determined, and we were hopeful that we would have our day. We were planting many seeds that had tremendous promise.

The year 2008 was not a great time to be a real estate agent. While homeownership changed hands, it often changed into the hands of the banks and not other buyers. The economy of those years ended in a steep decline that cost our family everything. My income dried up, and it appeared that there was no respite in our sights.

We declared bankruptcy, which means we lost our house, our cars, some of our possessions, and we even had to inventory our clothes to see if there was more that the courts could sell off to pay off our home. We weren't deep in debt, but we were at a loss to meet those demands due to an almost complete lack of income. I took work where I could find it, but income was hard to come by. I even worked from 2:00 to 8:00 am doing inbound phone sales for the "(Donald) Trump Wealth Builder-Blueprint" program. People would call in after hearing advertisements for the product on the radio. I talked to desperate people looking for a floatation device in the raging sea of a turbulent economy. People would, understandably, ask me on the phone, "If the product is so great and can make me so rich, why are you not using it to get out of your job in phone sales?" I either had to lie or tell them that wealth building takes time and to not see this product as a quick fix. Rarely did that line land me a sale, but at least I wasn't breaking moral standards. In an effort to be an honest salesman, I asked for and received a complimentary copy of the program to review for myself.

I answered phones hawking what ended up being a largely vague set of information on a set of audio CDs and a DVD that may or may not have helped people find forms of income. The first lesson of the wealth builder blueprint should have been, "Don't spend $400 on this product. If you bought this, you are going the wrong way." Years later I would try to sell the complimentary copy of the product on eBay, only to find out that no one wanted to even pay $2 for the set.

Inbound phone sales can be an alright job for the right person, but it wasn't for me. I would come home, shower and change, and go to the office to be a real estate agent for another 8 hours. But this was 2008. The market was crashing, and no one could get a loan anymore. In a commission only job, if no one is buying, no one is making commissions. My day involved doing my phone sales job, where I made enough to cover our food for the month and nothing more, then I would go to the office and fail for another 8 hours. This lifestyle was physically and emotionally exhausting. So I would come home after 15 hours of working to a messy home, and where daily chores and church assignments loomed.

During this time in our marriage, my wonderful spouse struggled through what we came to see as clinical depression (and at times) combined with progressively worsening postpartum depression. For my wife, depression was quite acute. Without resources to address the issue we both felt lost and hopeless. While she navigated marriage and family life as best she could while enduring almost crippling mental health challenges, I experienced my own difficult transformation. I transitioned from a place of comfort and normalcy, along with what could be considered a promising education and career path at the start of our married life, into a place of naivety, uncertainty, and emotional exhaustion. I felt little to no power to divert me from this downward spiral into increasing darkness.

My wife, as with many people experiencing clinical depression, had either no energy or lacked desire to be a part of the demands of reality. But we had children, a house to care and pay for, and other commitments— demands that did not offer respite. In many ways, I became a virtual-single parent. I did all the cooking, the cleaning, the work in and out of the home. Additionally, church responsibilities grew in ways that seemed to escalate the sense of chaos. In many ways, I had to raise our first three daughters (at that time) largely by myself. To compound these demands, I viewed my wife's depression as my fault—or at least my responsibility to "fix." She was sad because I was not able to provide. On top of that, I was hardly around because I was working. But work offered little reward. So, if I wasn't home, our children were neglected; if I wasn't at work, our income was neglected.

All around me was failure, as I saw it. I wasn't happy in my work, and I felt I was no good at it, hence no income. My wife was getting deeper into depression, which, I thought, was something I should be able to handle. Part of being a good husband was creating an environment in which his wife would naturally be happy. So if she wasn't happy, I was clearly failing. With the bankruptcy, we lost everything I tried to provide. So even the meager possessions we had earned up to that point were being taken, minus some clothes and some ability to cook whatever food we could get from Church welfare.

This sense of failure went on for years. While we were losing our house and I wrestled with the notion that we might just become homeless, two small tender mercies made their way into our life, even if by means of hardship to others. I decided it was time to get my degree and start back into doing sound engineering work to both provide for our family and to hold greater promise of employment in the future. Through a singular job opportunity I found a new line of work doing sound at conventions. The other tender mercy came when my sister and brother-in-law needed to move out of their home and needed someone to take over their payments for a time.

My older sister had moved into a home a couple years prior with her two kids and her husband, who was not a naturalized citizen of the United States. She was one of my few real estate clients during that time of sales drought. They sought to get his citizenship legalized around the same time that we lost our house. His application was denied, which meant they needed to move to Mexico for a ten-year waiting period. The housing market had just dropped out, which meant that they wouldn't be able to sell their house easily, so we moved in and took over the payments. While it was not the most positive of circumstances, without that happening our family would have not had a place to live. Renting to people who recently declared bankruptcy and have no job is not a tempting prospect for landlords. However, this would be a new start for our family, but it was also sort of a fix for my sister at the same time. The timing couldn't have worked out better for our family, even if it came at a time of trial for my sister's family.

Bankruptcy is a sort of "new start" in some ways, but only when it comes to debt. Bankruptcy can't wipe away the trauma or the emotional baggage that we packed up and moved to the new home with us. My wife was still depressed, we still had a rent payment to make, we still needed food, and we still needed the means to provide it. It didn't help that one week after we came to this new ward, I was called to be Young Men

President to a group of great young men, but who deserved a leader that wasn't trudging through the mire of three young children, a depressed wife, and no real income to speak of.

I tried my best to provide for the family. I took all the jobs I could get my hands on. I made tough decisions to find work that would be of a long-term benefit, not just something to make it through another month. We continued to have children, and my wife's postpartum continued to get worse. I was bound and determined to not fail again, but with the many expectations I would place on others and on opportunities that would come along, failure was hard to avoid.

I became desperate to self-medicate the pain and stress I felt due to the many areas where I felt an over-responsibility. Additionally, there was a growing sense of despair and failure in my abilities to fulfill the responsibilities of fatherhood and discipleship. In areas where I felt out of control in my personal life, or where I encountered anguish and reclusive sociality at home, I sought for relief by spending an increasing amount of time and effort on work outside of our home life. I served on city committees and on the community council for my children's school. All this in hopes of feeling some sense of productivity or positivity. I also did this to experience some sense of control and achievement during a time when I felt many things were crumbling around me. The dark cloud of feeling powerless to affect any change towards happiness was darkening my view of the future.

Life did start to come together a little bit more with each passing year. There were trials, but things were getting more and more stable as I fought to build a business that was providing a quality and valuable service. This business was doing sound work in the international language services industry (yes, that is a thing). I would work at conventions and business meetings all around the world. I love travel, and this job provided many ways for me to feel successful in that it was the best income our family had ever seen. It wasn't amazing, but given our history, we had learned to live on very little.

Heidi wanted to get her head out of the darkness and felt that she needed to have an outlet with the world. While depression wasn't gone, she was a fighter that mustered enough energy to engage with the world in ways she hadn't considered for years. By this time, our oldest daughter was turning 8 years old, which meant that she was of age to be baptized. As was somewhat of a tradition in our families, that was also the time when the child is given a set of scriptures as a baptism present. The scriptures produced by the Church came in a few color options at the time, so we asked our daughter which one she wanted: black, brown, green, or blue. She said she wanted pink. Figures. We thought that someone out there had to make pink scriptures. Such a popular color that would be with the girls—someone had to make them. Yet it didn't exist. No one made pink scripture covers!

In our research we saw people petitioning the Church in online forums to print pink scriptures, yet they didn't exist. So, my wife went to work to learn how to bind and rebind books so we could make our daughter pink scriptures. As we came to learn how to bind books at home, we wondered if we could put up a small website and take orders for other people wanting pink scriptures. We didn't have any expectation for what this would provide for our family. But if we got a call every now and then, wonderful! This would give Heidi something to do, and it could be the means of contributing financially.

Over time we developed an online business called Custom LDS Scriptures. My wife wanted it to be her business, nothing I would control. She needed and wanted to do this on her own. Having seen her in depression for years and waver in her ability, capacity, or desire to complete other things, I had my doubts. (Hint: It doesn't help people with depression to remind them of how their infirmity is reason to think that they may continue to fall short.)

I had seen my wife try things and not complete them, which seemed to send her further into depression. I felt I was saving her the pain of failing at something else by asserting myself more fully into the business. There were times when she was overwhelmed, and she invited me in to help. There were other times when my help was intrusive and made the situation worse. The more I would feel she was struggling, the more I would inject myself more fully into the business. I was trying to protect her from failing. However, when I did that, I was actually taking away her chance to feel in control. And when the business would be helped by my presence, it served as evidence that maybe she couldn't handle it.

The business kind of took off. We were getting orders almost daily. And for a product that takes two days to make, it is not hard to imagine how that work would pile up, leaving a wake of unhappy customers. So I would jump in to help get things caught up, but it was still me "saving" her from what I thought would be a depression-inducing failure. Over time, she did burn out—she felt that she wanted to walk away from the work that was eroding her happiness and keeping her from feeling a sense of accomplishment. The thing I feared was taking place. I didn't want to see something that had economic value, something that was actually getting sales and something that was desirable to the target customers, just fade away because she "quit" (as I saw it). So, I stepped in again to try and save it, and this time it was a full and official takeover.

I went to work with my business traveling and working conventions around the world, and I ran Custom LDS Scriptures. Two full-time businesses were my responsibility. For a whole year it was my goal to turn around Custom LDS Scriptures. I would fix the mess my wife had made of things (again, as I saw it). The last few months, Heidi virtually walked away from customers that had already given us money for a product. I wanted to see if I could make the business profitable and even something we could sell for a big chunk of change. On some level I was saving myself from turning down an opportunity for money. Why? How much I would have loved to have a business that was making money back when we had to declare bankruptcy!

In the meantime I would also be saving my wife from seeing something she built and worked hard on for years just fizzle out. I feared what that would do to her mentality, and I feared what it would do to our finances. I determined that I would save the day, I would provide for the family, and I would save my wife from feeling like a failure! What a win...or so I thought.

Yes, I did rehab the business; yes, we had a great year of sales; and it was successfully sold to people that are doing an amazing job with the business. The new owners do truly incredible work, and it has provided and produced well for their family. We couldn't be happier for them. On the surface, the effort accomplished what it set out to do. We needed the money, we sold the business, problems resolved. Only one issue still remained: there was still depression, only now it was fueled by some resentment on my part. For a whole year I crushed myself, running two businesses, along with Church callings, I was a dad to five girls, and oh yeah, I was still doing a vast majority of the household chores.

This wasn't about my wife contributing or not contributing, or even being a mother who did this or that. The imbalance was that I came to realize, again, that my value to my family seemed to be in what I provided for them. The more "stuff" they had, the more evidence I had that I was a provider. I was out to prove that I wasn't a failure as I had been with the bankruptcy. The easier my wife had access to comfort and things that brought her joy, as well as keeping her away from unpleasant things (which is what Custom LDS Scriptures became), the better I was at being a husband. These were the same issues that I had been battling for almost a decade now.

While my wife was going through depression, since before we moved to Utah, and in the decade that followed, I did what I could to fight for the ideal. If my wife couldn't contribute to a clean house because she was so depressed that she sat in bed reading or sleeping all day, that's okay,

I would do it. If we needed dinner and my wife had no desire to cook anything, no problem, I had it. When our kids needed toys, I would do what I could to get toys. Nothing illegal of course, but I saw their needs as my responsibility. This went on for the first 15 years of our marriage, escalating in scope and in the burden it was creating.

Everything I was feeling burdened with was compounded by what I will affectionately refer to as the costs of discipleship. During these previous years I was a gospel doctrine teacher, a Young Men president, a counselor in our ward's elders quorum presidency (to three different presidents), executive secretary, and Sunday School president. I produced podcasts (on demand internet radio) that focused on defending The Church of Jesus Christ of Latter-day Saints and building faith for those who experienced what is often described as a faith crisis. I tried to visit local members of the Church but felt the guilt that came with falling short of that effort. I sought to participate in every Saturday morning move-in or move-out, as well as other service opportunities in the area. I served that two-year service mission with LDS Family Services as an audiovisual missionary developing training videos on a variety of topics centered around mental health. This was all on top of the demands to work full time and provide all financial resources. I came to a point where my heart was failing me, and I began to fear what the rest of my life would present. In short, I was being crushed by the weight of the world, as well as the demands I felt from my Church obligations.

This list of efforts is not mentioned as a way of bragging, rather an illustration of the unhealthy and debilitating choices that slowly led me down a path towards burnout and resentment. I also mention these things because to the outside world, I appear a faithful, active member of The Church of Jesus Christ of Latter-day Saints. While I do consider myself to be a faithful and active member, I am not sure that I was practicing my faith in the healthiest way possible.

I don't regret all the service I rendered for good, not for one minute. And these choices on the surface don't sound like negative things to avoid. After all, I felt I was trying to be a caring husband, a diligent providing father, and an active member of the Church. But when I looked at my life, I began to wonder if what I was doing was not as selfless as I thought it was, or if all my efforts were meant to make me feel good during a time when I felt lost, and tired. Was I doing good or was doing things that appeared good but ultimately left me unfulfilled due to selfish motivations. Additionally, I started to regret many things in my life because I began to feel they had been "demanded" of me, or at least expected of me to the degree that I felt that I had no choice. I was no longer choosing to be good, but was expected to be everything good for everyone, all the time.

Along the way, I bought into the notion that I had to be spiritual enough for both me and my wife—because if I was spiritual enough, God would have to bless my wife to get better. When I saw others who were struggling with their faith, with their family life, or with whatever challenge they were experiencing, I would sweep in to try to fix them or their situation—because if I fixed others, maybe I could be fixed too. I knew the depth of pain and stress I was experiencing, and I desperately didn't want anyone else to go through the same pain. At times, I would see the trials of others as somehow being my responsibility to fix.

On the surface, this may have appeared to be a good thing; after all I was serving others and was bolstering people who needed help in a time of trial. The reality was that I began to resent people for those very things. I resented marrying my wife, who was supposed to help me achieve greater happiness and fulfillment but who had become a burden and anchor (as I saw it at the time). I viewed those who had a faith crisis with disdain because I felt they were making their personal choices public (via blogs and other means) in an attempt to make their personal faith challenges someone else's responsibility to fix. People in pain often cry out for people to fix their problems for them. Rather than feeling compassion and selflessness, I felt this self-imposed burden to resolve the dissonance they were feeling. After all, if I didn't, I was a bad person for not even trying. On the other hand, if I did, I was being the world's doormat. In my view of things, these were the only two options.

This conflict fertilized a sense of discontent and a dissonance in my mind and heart. But what could I do? I had been raised to be compassionate, to serve, and to "mourn with those that mourn"[3]—to be saviors on Mount Zion.[4] I would read that Jesus Christ, our Savior and exemplar, took on the sins of the world and so many of our other burdens through his grace and Atonement. If he is our Savior, and we are supposed to be saviors on Mount Zion, shouldn't I be carrying other people's burdens? Over time, I came to realize that Jesus Christ chose his path: he was no victim, regardless of how it may look in the movies and paintings.

I felt as if I had become a slave to these Christian ideals rather than choosing them. I desperately wanted to choose Christian discipleship even if it was on the off chance that I would actually feel the peace and rest the gospel promises to the valiant. Rather than feeling rewarded for doing good, I resented my acts, feeling that charity had been unjustly demanded of me. Seeing charity as a burden rather than a choice stole from me the chance to be the disciple I desperately wanted to be.

In all that I experienced I still felt unable to find answers to what was happening in my own life and the life of my eternal companion, which only added to the confusion. Why was I feeling the way I was, and why was my spouse stuck and unable to find answers to her depression? To a certain extent, I wondered why I had felt a loss of happiness in spite of all the scriptural and prophetic promises of joy for those who kept the commandments of the Lord? Is this a question that has an answer?

While I had learned much about various challenges from mental health issues during my time as a service missionary for LDS Family Services, I had never heard the one word that perfectly described what I was experiencing, and what I would begin to see around me and in a great many others—codependency.

After years of struggle there came a point in our marriage where I either needed to see a therapist that would help me learn to cope with her depression and our situation, or something else would result. I didn't see divorce as an option, but I also didn't know what to call the next steps we would face. I wasn't planning for that future, nor was I interesting in what that would look like. The inevitability of that eventual reality scared me to my core. With some prayer, Heidi and I decided on a therapist with whom we would engage in our last ditch effort to save our lives and marriage.

After the first couple of months of trying we started to see a light and the end of the tunnel. Heidi was smiling again, and I began to feel a weight lifting off my shoulders. As she "got better" I would start to feel better too. While this sounds like a good thing, and it was for Heidi, I came to realize how my happiness was dependent on the world the around me. After Heidi's depression was managed and largely out of the picture, I realized it was time for me to get better.

Therapy helped save our marriage. It wasn't that God was insufficient, or that our faith was lacking. But we feel that God places certain people and certain trials in our path to provide us with experiences that teach us things in ways that we would not obtain in another way. A therapist's knowledge and years of experience can be a gift brought to bear through certain trails. "God does notice us, and he watches over us. But it is usually through another person that he meets our needs. Therefore, it is vital that we serve each other."[5]

Simply put, we had things we needed to learn, and it was time that we learned them. In order for us to progress and be a part of God's work, we needed to get ourselves right. We are partners with God in His work to exalt us. That means we must put in some work as well. There should be no expectation of magic wands that grant us the wishes of our hearts simply because we think we are good people. Therapy can be a divine work that helps us come to realize a better version of ourselves—but it is work.

My wife, Heidi, overcame her depression through a practice called EMDR. I have continued in therapy, including CBT, EMDR, and Brainspotting[6] to help address my ongoing codependency. While we are far better off than just a few short years ago, we recognize there is more work to be done. It has not been an easy task, and we both feel the need to keep checking back in from time to time with professional help. More importantly we are working with each other to help the other through these challenges. We both have grown individually, in our marriage, and in our relationship to our faith, in light of these challenges.

Disclaimers

Before introducing the subject of codependency, we need to offer some words of caution. The words of Jacob, a brother of Nephi in the Book of Mormon, can be employed with new meaning, "O be wise; what can I say more?" (Jacob 6:12). Navigating what is presented secularly on this subject and reconciling it with the doctrine of the Church is a nuanced but enlightening pursuit. While many secular concepts on codependency have their spiritually principled counterpart, some do not. Sifting through both inspired and secular information can be confusing. The goal in this text is to help distill the information necessary to recognize the symptomatic behaviors and move towards resolving codependency in our lives and discipleship.

Over the course of reading any text dealing with codependency (including websites and articles), one can easily jump to impulsive judgment. This is understandable. But quickly finding information and then prescribing treatment based on a narrow understanding should be done with caution, if done at all. Misdiagnosing and applying the wrong remedy can be as dangerous as not treating the ailment in the first place. We will ask questions of the reader from time to time. These questions are meant to be self-reflective, not self-convicting, so as to help you apply the material to your own circumstance.

As with anything relating to health issues, be it mental, physical, or emotional, no one should fully self-diagnose strictly by reading one text. It is the wisdom and skill of thoughtful and skilled therapists that help many rise from the ashes of mental health challenges and who have the skills to address codependency recovery efforts. As you become familiar with information on codependency, you can better be in tune with courses of action that may or may not require professional assistance. Please do not dismiss or even undervalue the skills of trained therapists and mental health professionals in your effort to combat codependency.

Codependency, like clinical depression, anxiety, or other mental health issues are not to be feared or considered a life sentence. Trained professionals, as well as connecting you with a caring and understanding support system, can be a very beneficial force in combating your codependency. Elder Scott D. Whiting offers this encouragement, "Now, those of us who are brave might consider asking a trusted family member, spouse, friend, or spiritual leader what attribute of Jesus Christ we are in need of—and we may need to brace ourselves for the response! Sometimes we see ourselves with distorted fun-house mirrors that show us either much more round or much more lean than we really are. Trusted friends and family can help us see ourselves more accurately, but even they, as loving and helpful as they would like to be, can see things imperfectly. As a result, it is vital that we also ask our loving Heavenly Father what we are in need of and where we should focus our efforts. He has a perfect view of us and will lovingly show us our weakness."

It is true that over the course of life we all will experience moments, if not prolonged periods, where we display the symptoms of what will be presented. Feeling some connection to what is presented is not a sign that one is "diagnosed." When individuals come to learn about health-related issues it is not uncommon to overly pathologize—or to overly diagnose.[7] Spiritual and emotional hypochondriacs may result from misinterpreting this text or others like it.

The intent of learning is not to be reactionary to the things we learn or to be at the mercy of information. We are to digest, internalize, and prioritize knowledge in a way that encourages self-mastery and exalting actions.

Alright, now that the disclaimer matters are out of the way, let's begin.

CHAPTER I – DEFINING CODEPENDENCY

Introduction to Codependency

Each of us lives hundreds of simultaneous lives--each life created
and played out in the mind of those with whom we have a relationship.
Who we are, or what our life is perceived to be, is different to each person
and colored by the nature of each relationship. But who we perceive
ourselves to be in our own life is a journey into self-discovery that many
have only just begun. This journey is filled with both peril and triumph,
confusion and enlightenment. Like reading scriptures, or a classic text, we
can view our own lives and relationships differently based on where we are
at in our journey. Context and experience will illuminate part of our lives
in a way that is both instructive and humbling. With each of the many
relationships we have, we can learn something about ourselves that will
propel us forward on our journey. When reviewing some of our
relationships we may come to learn our "life" is so entirely absorbed in the

1

choices and consequences of others that we no longer see the unique person we are supposed to be. When our journey feels like it is no longer our story, or where we are the side character of everyone else's story, our soul begins to mourn the loss of self, fading away from its divinely appointed potential. This is codependency.

Codependency is a name or title that can be misleading as to its proper meaning. Originally a term used to describe those connected by way of relationship to an individual deemed an alcoholic, codependency has been expanded to include many other types of unhealthy behaviors, emotional responses, and relationships. The secular definition of codependency continues to evolve and be understood. As a result, some have been cautious or even offended by the notion that they may be experiencing some degree of codependency.

After discovering the complex concept of codependency in a secular setting, our next step will be to see how this set of behaviors can lead to codependent discipleship with God, with the Church, and with our family-based religious experiences. And in fact, as we will see, unexamined codependency has devastating consequences for families, church communities, and one's own spiritual character. For those of us who have struggled in this area, sometimes we have to deal with this before we can more fully, and more joyfully, follow the teachings of the scriptures, the

Church, and the prophet. Our goal here is to help you find clarity in this area so that your spiritual life can be more life-giving. If codependency is a stumbling block on the covenant path, then let's figure out how to remove it so that our journey on the path continues.

What Is Codependency?

Diagnosis of mental health conditions is not like answering a math problem. Many variables exist that can remain hidden or well guarded, while others are simply too fluid to efficiently quantify. The lived experience of an individual is complex to measure, and the "answer" to a given set of symptoms is therefore difficult to determine. For this reason, even if individuals at times experience symptoms of codependency, this does not mean that an individual is considered a codependent. The adage can apply: *Just because someone sneezes, doesn't mean they have a cold.* However, when one does show the signs, it is best to be mindful of what those apparent similarities might suggest.

There has been a movement to include codependency in the canon[8] of mental health since the mid-80s but, as you will soon learn, it's a difficult diagnosis to make. What looks like codependency in one situation is absolutely not in another. However, there are principles that can guide

3

the discussion. Discovering mental health issues is about recognizing patterns, understanding why they are occurring, and deciding how to move forward. For the codependent person, this can be both empowering and terrifying.

Whatever you have heard, or what you think the word codependency might imply, we would invite you to park those preconceived notions while reading this text. The label might be misleading, and your thoughts about who or what circumstances produce codependency could be incomplete or misguided. So to make sure we are on the same page, let's start from the beginning.

Historical Definitions

The original concept of codependence came into being as a way to describe the behaviors of individuals who had an established relationship with a chemical dependency. The codependent was typically a spouse, and most commonly the wife of a husband who was an alcoholic. In these scenarios, the wife who loved her husband deeply also found that she felt a sense of duty or responsibility to fix the problems created in the destructive wake of her husband's addiction-fueled behavior. After months or years of trying to repair and even apologize for the behavior of her husband, the wife would develop what became the earliest definition of codependency.

Codependency is typically defined by a distinct set of persistent behaviors, including a set of choices, *that become an addiction* in its own way. This set includes taking on the burdens of others, thus defining this person as a sort of "reactionary savior" due to the actions, misdeeds, tragedies, or trials of others for whom they feel responsible. These behaviors may seem normal at first, perhaps even healthy when observed casually. But, when viewed through the lens of codependency, these same behaviors can shift and be characterized as an unhealthy response to the choices of others.

Emotional mismanagement of reactions to a number of scenarios can fertilize the seeds of codependency. This can happen even when an individual becomes compelled by a sense of duty, or even genuine charity, but ends up assuming responsibility for the actions or consequences of others and becomes the remedy to those actions in the process. While this is a sort of quick and short definition, there are others that can be helpful in understanding the topic on a more empowering level.

The many definitions of codependency may leave a person thinking that it is so vague that it is both nothing and everything at the same time. In order to best cut through that mess, we will summarize a few of the better secular definitions that have been offered:

Codependency is a type of dysfunctional helping relationship where one person supports or enables another person's drug addiction, alcoholism, gambling addiction, poor mental health, immaturity, irresponsibility, or under-achievement by removing or fixing the consequences others experience. In its broadest definition, a codependent is someone who cannot function from their innate self and whose thinking and behavior is instead organized around another person, or even a process, or substance.

(Take a deep breath, and internalize that definition. When you are ready, continue.)

Codependency has been referred to as the disease of a lost self. Codependent relationships are partially defined by intimacy problems, dependency, denial, dysfunctional communication and boundaries, and high reactivity. Often, there is a perceived imbalance in the relationship. Some codependents often find themselves in relationships where their primary role is that of rescuer, supporter, and confidante. These helper types are often dependent on the other person's poor functioning to satisfy their own emotional needs. Many codependents place a lower priority on their own needs, while being excessively preoccupied with the needs of others. Codependency can occur in any type of relationship, including family, work, friendship, and also romantic, peer or community relationships.

(Okay, got that? There is a lot to take in. If you need to read it twice, go ahead. No one will know.)

DO ANY OF THESE CHARACTERISTICS SEEM TO BE PRESENT SOMEWHERE IN YOUR LIFE OR IN THE LIFE OF SOMEONE YOU KNOW?

There is one key factor that lies at the heart of what separates codependency from what would otherwise be viewed as an admirable quality: when the behavior can be deemed as "excessive and unhealthy, even uncontrollable." Meaning, there can come a point where people do the right things for the wrong reasons, or perhaps they feel as if they have no choice in their actions, even if those actions appear outwardly kind. With codependency, the line is often, if not compulsively, crossed where personal health and well-being are compromised and therefore defined as charity.

The current discussions on codependency and its developing definition does not require an individual to be connected to something or someone that is classified as dependent in order to qualify. Just because the word codependent has the prefix of "co," meaning joined with or partnered with someone or something, doesn't actually require the thing for which a person is codependent to also be dependent. Perhaps that makes codependency a bit of a misnomer to some, hence the controversy. The name is still fitting because the codependent person treats or views people or things as if they are dependent. In short, codependency can be one-sided.

Codependency is typically found in a relationship to a human being but can also be fostered by unhealthy perspectives on things, conditions, or even circumstances. Much like a drug addict finds different ways to divert responsibility for his life or pursues paths of avoidance as a means of self-medicating emotional pain or disappointment, codependents will self-medicate by becoming attached to different things that "need" them or things that they can fix. These objects of obsession can be their job, a pet, or even a smartphone. Sometimes an individual can be codependent towards someone or something that is innocuous or perhaps even perfectly healthy. Again, codependency does not actually require a second party with dependency to qualify. However, codependency is more likely to be the result of a relationship where there is some dysfunction or brokenness with which a person can be the rescuer or defender.

Part of the nuance here is that the codependent person BENEFITS from the other being sick/needy/broken. Think of a family with three teenage siblings, where one is an addict. The other two siblings would be telling the truth when they say that they very much want their sibling to get better. But there is reality to the idea that they benefit in some related ways due to the presence of their sibling's disease. Maybe Mom and Dad let things slide with them a little bit more; or maybe they feel better about themselves because they are not addicted; or maybe they like being seen by society as the good kid in the family, even if they only appear so when compared to their addicted sibling.

So the codependent person is in a difficult spot because they truly do want to help that person—and if they do, the secondary gains they receive because of the other's problems go away. It's the ultimate in ambivalence: "I want you to get better, but I get scared when you get better."

For example, a codependent spouse doesn't necessarily have a relationship with their spouse's alcohol, but with the spouse. However, as will be shown later in this text, codependency isn't the relationship itself, but the behaviors present in certain relationships to people or things.

Individuals will always have something they determine as a need. When that person places the responsibility of fulfilling that need on another, they are classified as a dependent; at least in that thing for which they are dependent. This is true of children and is considered an appropriate and legally justifiable state given their developmental stage. This is especially true with newborns and younger children. Dependency can be acutely experienced in cases of individuals with special needs, such as some cases of autism, physical or developmental disabilities, and other complex health-related issues. The needs of these children can become a drain on most parents to the point that they no longer feel that they are giving of their time in their care, but time is taken from them, stolen or demanded. Dependency can be based on an addiction, be it chemical or psychological, but it can also simply be part of one's mortal experience.

The perfect storm for codependency can be found in the following scenario:

A dependent person may communicate the following message, "I have an anxious or bad feeling, and I need you to make me feel better regardless of how busy or unavailable you are." The codependent will then respond, "I resent you putting this on me, especially when I am not able to deal with my own issues, but I also need to resolve this issue or I won't feel complete, useful, or needed. I will fix this, so this problem goes away."

Codependents often need broken people around them to feel value, and if they are not fixing other people, they will feel empty and without purpose.

HOW DO YOU VALUE YOURSELF? HOW MUCH OF HOW YOU SEE YOURSELF IS BASED ON HOW MUCH OTHER PEOPLE NEED YOU?

This is where codependents have much in common with people who have an eating disorder.[9] One can't eliminate their need for food, nor can codependents eliminate their need for other people entirely. These behaviors are reactive, and they hope to medicate a perceived pain. They are also compulsory and serve in a similar way as do other addictive behaviors. Not only does this response enable the dependent, but it gives meaning and therefore an emotional benefit or "high" to the codependent.

A codependent often feels that they have to save people from many of the negative consequences of life, or even the consequences of their perceived dependency and victimization by others. Eventually this also leads to emotional exhaustion in the codependent that creates a cycle of dependency. So, as the codependent rescues others to the point of depletion, they then feel guilty when they recognize they need saving, too. Then they feel guilty for putting others in the position of saving, feeling that they are perpetuating the pain of dependency. Codependents may long for the day when people don't "need" them, but also find tremendous challenge in even visualizing their life without being surrounded by people who need them.

A more current understanding of codependency

For a more complete and current definition of codependency we need to understand that "codependency does not refer to all caring behavior or feelings, but only those that are excessive to an unhealthy degree."[10] One of the distinctions is that healthy empathy and caregiving is motivated by conscious choice, whereas codependents' actions are compulsive. To keep this definition within reasonable boundaries it is safe to say that codependency is an over-responsibility that manifests as positive impulses that have become out of control. Responsibility for relationships with others must coexist with responsibility to oneself.[11]

Codependency is partially defined as having an element of persistence or something experienced over an extended period of time. Single acts might fit the behavior-based criteria of a codependent act but do not qualify a person as being a codependent or as having codependency. Patterns of behavior that dictate one's choices take time to present themselves or to be considered a pathological behavior. When an individual is showing consistent signs for over a month and a half to three months, maybe even over a year, this could be a sign to consider the likelihood of codependency.

If symptoms develop due to a trauma or life event and symptoms present themselves, this doesn't mean that someone has codependency. However, traumatic events or trying circumstances can be a catalyst for developing such persistent behaviors as means of self-medicating.[12]

There are token phrases that are uttered, though sometimes silently, by the "textbook" codependent. "I will be happy when (insert name) gets better or stops doing (insert behavior)." Another common codependent approach to life is, "When others fix themselves, then I can fix myself." The individual's life is held in some kind of happiness escrow until this other set of external conditions are met. Relinquishing our own happiness to some external locus of control is a dangerous and largely unfulfilling existence that involves "loving our broken and destructive neighbor" while making ourselves hostages until that is accomplished.

When an individual's happiness is dependent on an external change taking place or as a prerequisite to happiness, there is a likelihood that codependency is present or will develop. In the case of the wife of an alcoholic husband, she will see her life and her happiness as contingent on the actions and choices of an addict. This pattern of behavior is likely to leave her feeling trapped, depressed, and at a loss of identity separate from the negative behaviors of those by whom she feels victimized. "If you can't regulate your own emotional temperature, you'll regulate everyone around you to keep yourself comfortable."[13]

While the individual looking to do the saving may feel properly motivated, it is largely done with very little consideration as to whether that effort is actually healthy for the person being "saved" or if it is even wanted or needed. Codependent acts tend to be impulsive. By that definition, codependents often "fix" where there is no need or where "fixing" can actually make things worse. In a world of emotional littering, codependents are picking up the mess and carrying garbage bags overflowing with other people's problems.

———————◆———————

DO PEOPLE NEED FIXING? DO I NEED TO BE THE ONE
THAT FIXES THEM? HOW WOULD MY RELATIONSHIP
CHANGE IF I DIDN'T VIEW THAT PERSON AS BROKEN
AND IN NEED OF FIXING?

———————◆———————

Similar symptoms but different diagnosis

Dependent Personality Disorder (DPD)

Dependent Personality Disorder (DPD) is a close cousin to codependency but is distinctly different. DPD is not where an individual needs to save others, to help others, or to control their environment. Someone with DPD must be saved or taken care of, and this need is underscored by feeling a need to be submissive to others out of a fear of separation. DPD is often accompanied by a fear of being abandoned and tends to have a familial or hereditary component. While similar, these two should be approached differently from a therapeutic standpoint and often have different causes.

There is a version of codependency where the neediness of dependency appears to be in the driver's seat. A codependency that leads with dependency is still about controlling another person—it's just trying to control them into being the perfect husband, friend, or boss.

Low Self-Esteem

Low self-esteem occurs when an individual feels little to no self-worth or that they have no value to others. This can be the result of aesthetic matters (such as weight or baldness) or other areas where the individual regards their part in the world as of little consequence. While acknowledging low self-esteem can be a part of diagnosing codependency, it doesn't mean that when one has low-self esteem they automatically experience codependency: they are not cause and effect. Much like DPD, low self-esteem is similar enough to codependency that it is not uncommon to see these issues talked about as the "same thing" even though they are distinct by definition.

Low self-esteem can be a contributing factor in that individuals may seek to create codependent relationships as an attempt at feeling some sense of value and purpose. This argument has been presented as an explanation for individuals who almost habitually seek out destructive or corrosive relationships with those who could be categorized as being dependent for one reason or another. With low self-esteem, it may be an initiating factor, or the reason that codependency continues, but they are not one and the same.

Different diagnosis require different remedies

A headache can have many causes and as a result be benefited by different remedies. Ibuprofen, Naproxen, and Acetaminophen all can help with headache or pain symptoms, but they address the pain in different ways due to different causes. As a result, each treatment can be more or less effective than others. Different underlying causes receive best care when first identified and then treated accordingly. Similarly, it is best to address codependency or its similar diagnosis with different forms of care.

A good practice is to ensure that codependency is not being compounded by other issues—if it is codependency at all. Diagnosis and other best practices often take someone either of tremendous experience and study, or better yet, someone with sufficient formal education and clinical experience to navigate this nuanced issue. We reiterate that we use the term diagnose here to mean something less than *clinical*, but is still the process by which we determine how to proceed.

Words of caution

It is not uncommon for people once they are introduced to this topic to begin seeing "the signs" or conclude that they are now an expert. This is particularly true for those who find these concepts resonate with their own experience. After all, if you have been codependent for years and just now figured out what has been going on, it's easy to assume that your years of lived experience give you a master's degree on the subject. Please be careful to not "play" therapist. While that temptation is real, it also takes years of study, and experience with codependency to put this subject into perspective. It is our hope that by coming to a basic understanding of codependency, our ability to be properly empathetic with others and to develop the Healer's art will be enlarged.

Self-Assessment for Codependency

Where does one draw that line between healthy and unhealthy behaviors when they are, in essence, the same outward behavior? Therein lies the challenge and the reason that so many so often cross that line into codependency without knowing. People can understandably be confused about codependency.

Following is a series of questions you can ask yourself to help determine if an act is codependent:

- What is my motivation?

- Am I doing _____ because I made a conscious choice to do it, or am I acting from guilt and obligation?

- Am I choosing to give of my time, or resources? or am I giving compulsively without thinking about what I'm doing?

- Am I hoping someone will like or love me if I do or give something to her or him?

- Do I personally feel lovable and likable, and do I have self-esteem? Or do I have to prove those things to other people and myself?

- How do I feel when I _____? Do I feel resentful? Used? Victimized? Or do I feel comfortable with and responsible for my choices?"

In a clinical setting, a therapist may ask the following of an individual showing signs of codependency:

- What legitimate need are you trying to meet? (To feel connection? To assuage anxiety? To avoid chaos?)
- Who is responsible for meeting that need?
- What can you do to help yourself meet that legitimate need?
- Are you able to meet your own need without acting out codependently, thus controlling or damaging your relationship with others?

It is important to coach the mind to see that a codependent has legitimate needs underneath their codependency.[14] There is little value in diminishing these underlying needs as a coping mechanism. Acknowledging these needs can help to legitimize the rational aspects of what they are feeling, while also discovering healthier approaches to managing those needs. It is important to realize that each individual is (most often) the one responsible for meeting their own needs. This may not happen immediately. There will still be a need to learn patience and, to a certain extent, tolerate the feelings they are trying to avoid (shame, guilt, anger, etc.). However, in time, codependency is manageable, and recovery is a worthy pursuit.

Real Life Example of Codependency

It is one thing to have a grasp on the textual concept of codependency. It is quite another to understand how it looks in real life. Codependency is no respecter of economics, gender, or any other circumstance in which we may find ourselves. Examples can be found all around us. Here is one example of codependency from a mother who truly cares for her child:

Ashley (not her real name) is a fun-loving, kind woman in her mid-30s. She is mother to an eight-year-old son with a number of developmental challenges, autism being the most dominant of the diagnosed conditions. Since birth, her child presented with behaviors that confused and confounded most medical professionals who saw him. At first these challenges were a frustrating mystery, but they eventually developed into a straw taxing the proverbial camel's back. Before the initial diagnosis of autism was made, there were nights when Ashley and her husband would stay up all hours of the night wondering what was causing their child to have a never-ending supply of energy. Was he being fed wrong? Was there something wrong with their parenting style? Self-doubt gave way to the desire to find ways to "control" the enigmatic situation.

After diagnosis was pronounced and confirmed by multiple doctors came numerous follow-up doctor visits and learning to accept and adapt to a new lifestyle. Ashley's life was changed forever. Not only did she mourn the death of a life she wished for herself and for her son, but she needed to find a way to move forward with a clearer understanding of the obligations that would be her constant companion.

Ashley knew she loved her child, but she couldn't help but think that she was so consumed in the child's care that she was losing who she was as a person and began to lose her perceived value as a human being. Enslaved, as she saw it, by the compulsion to be a caring mother who met the endless demands that her child required, Ashley saw very little value in herself or enjoyment in her life. This child slowly turned from being a challenging but beautiful individual to a life sentence. Guilt became her second-most present emotion next to fatigue, because "what kind of person feels resentment towards something their child cannot control?"

To add complexity to this already demanding scenario, Ashley's neighbors in her apartment complex would come by and take advantage of what they would see as Ashley's generous and kind outward expressions—the person Ashley wanted to be, again. They would come and ask for a half-gallon of milk or a cup of laundry detergent—a simple and understandable request of civilized neighbors, or so it would seem. This pattern of neighbors asking Ashley for things started under the guise of "I need milk, but I don't have time to go to the store just now. Can I borrow some?" But, over time, as Ashley would oblige, this pattern of asking for goods or even her time escalated to the point that she was being taken advantage of. People knew she wouldn't say "no" because they assumed she was a good person, and because she considered herself a good person Ashley felt she couldn't say "no." After all, good people can't say "no" to serving one another.

For Ashley, even attending Church became a struggle. Church is a place where people with various struggles can come to find direction in the fellowship of others. Many at church knew of Ashley's typically bubbly character and saw her as an understanding and at times infectious, positive spirit. As emotionally dependent people usually do, they use others as a "responsibility garbage dump." So many would come to her asking for help or to just vent their problems because she was a good listener. Each time someone would come to her with a personal problem, she felt that she needed to fix or take on their problems.

At some point Ashley felt that people were largely selfish and that they needed to take care of their own problems, but even thinking that made her feel callous and cold. Going to Sunday School or Relief Society class meant having to talk to people–people who *might* need something of her. And because she knew what it felt like to have people dumping their problems on her, the last thing she wanted to do was go to class and dump her problems on them (especially if their behavior was part of the problem). It became a cycle of exponential stresses, and it became hard for her to know who was a genuine friend and who was just another person who needed something *from* her.

This saying seems appropriate: "Some people aren't loyal to you, they are loyal to their need of you. Once their needs change, so does their loyalty." So it was with Ashley and those who would drain her emotionally through their "need" of her kindness and positive outward energy.

People began to expect Ashley to be more than just an understanding sympathetic ear, but to be their rescuer. It is one thing to share, empathize, and even mourn with others. But to share and communicate trials for the sake of placing the responsibility on others to

24

fix their problems is a different set of unhealthy behaviors. For Ashley, it was hard to have the boundary in place to establish that line clearly for herself and for others.

These instances became so constant that Ashley felt she had nothing left to give, but she also felt guilty for not being able to help those who would come to her with their "needs." She felt a compulsion to be helpful, but then felt guilty because she didn't have the emotional stamina to keep giving when her own needs were not being met. She began to be defined as a problem solver—emotionally and, in some cases, economically.

Eventually, Ashley had "nothing left in the tank." Her emotional reservoir had run dry, and her inability to be the person she wanted caused her to change. Instead of being the helpful person she wanted to be, she would lock the door and not answer when people knocked. Some days she wouldn't even go to church for fear that someone, anyone, would "need" her for something. She didn't answer the phone when her family members would call because they too needed so much from her, more than she could give. It became easier to shut out the world than to meet the demands she felt were being placed on her.

To make this already volatile situation worse, Ashley began to define herself as a helper/rescuer. She felt that if she didn't live up to that expectation she would be seen as a disappointment, even a selfish person. So, when she locked her doors and closed off from the world, she felt lost, as if she were of no worth because she wasn't helping others. This cycle of helping, then crashing, would develop into a pattern that was emotionally eroding. Slowly, her choices were washing away the person she knew she could be—and the person she desperately wanted to become once more.

Her husband would try to tell her to not be so available, to establish and set boundaries with people, and to learn to say "no." But codependency is tricky. Helping others is often the drug of choice. Like addicts of other types, codependents feel pain in a powerful way. For codependents, the next "hit" comes by helping someone, rescuing someone, and then receiving their reward from the praise that they get from helping. This assurance tends to fade over time, and the high of being charitable is replaced by the guilt of not doing enough for someone else. Like other addictions, the demand for that high increases over time. In cases of codependency, individuals will push themselves to the brink of emotional overdose before they recognize the high is controlling their behavior. It's a debilitating cycle that seems to have no end.

Ashley was introduced by her home teachers to the watershed book on codependency by Melody Beattie, *Codependent No More: How to Stop Controlling Others and Start Caring for Yourself.*[15] After reading the book,

Ashley started to see the end results of where her life was heading. She realized her patterns of behavior and began to make incremental changes. Even small adjustments were life giving! Ashley was better able to manage her guilt, and she is still working on separating what she has control over and what she is not required to manage. Her experience is common, but it is an example of how codependency, the over-responsibility of certain relationships, can have a negative impact on individuals and families.

Like Ashley's scenario, codependent situations are not necessarily the result of spiritual sin or due to the presence of traditional forms of addiction. Ashley's over-responsibility was simply the result of an inability to act independently in her circumstances. As in Ashley's example, where there is dependency, codependency is made probable. Where one is surrounded with dependency, codependency seems almost inevitable.

If Ashely were a client sitting in a therapy session, the very first thing asked could be: Whose approval are you trying to earn, and what is keeping you hooked into this? Is it your neighbor, your church family, your husband? God? Your bishop? Your friends? Your mother's voice in your head? Where are you getting an "emotional high" for doing all of this?

One could continue to analyze what secondary benefit is Ashley getting. The most effective approach would be to explore Ashley's behavior toward her needy friends, but primarily address the fact that Ashley is hooked into this behavior because she is getting some kind of emotional payoff. While this may sound taxing (and it usually is), one's relationship with the emotional payoffs needs to be addressed.

Chapter 2 – Spiritual Codependency

"THE BEST AND MOST CLEAR INDICATOR THAT WE
ARE PROGRESSING SPIRITUALLY AND COMING UNTO
CHRIST IS THE WAY WE TREAT OTHER PEOPLE."

Marvin J. Ashton

———————◆———————

Human nature has not changed since the days of Adam and Eve, nor have any new emotions been invented. While there is no scripture, ancient or modern, that uses the term codependency, the concept is not new. There are warnings and counsel that help fend off codependency, but one must take on a new lens to see how eternal doctrines apply.

Codependency has the ability to infect many aspects of our lives and relationships. Codependency could be considered, justifiably, as a mortal condition that can impact our eternal souls. Because it is a pollution of what we might otherwise view as charitable impulses, it would be valuable to have an understanding of the ways this issue manifests in matters of Christian discipleship. The impulse toward charity is good, but codependency can be seen as a kind of counterfeit charity, not the charity that is the pure love of Christ.

Spiritual codependency may not be a clinical term or a diagnosis. But the idea that members of The Church of Jesus Christ of Latter-day Saints can suffer from a charity-dependent identity that can at times cause crippling guilt and over-responsibility for the salvation of others is a very real possibility. While understandable, this sort of character is not the ideal.

In order to address spiritual codependency, or codependent discipleship, in the proper spirit, we must be willing to be, as Neal A. Maxwell counseled, "sufficiently careful of the pain in people's lives. There are scars that go unnoticed, but [we] must see them. [We] must tread with caution on the hallowed ground of another's suffering."[16] Accordingly, David F. Holland postulated, "[Mental illness] is the next great frontier of our [latter-day] ministry."[17] Understanding codependency is a beginning step on a pioneering trek into the frontier of our contemporary ministering effort.

We are asserting something bold: mental health issues influence our spiritual character. This is a complex undertaking. For some this also implies that spiritual difficulties can be resolved through mental health modalities. We recognize the need for caution in mixing the learning of the world with the teachings of the divine; however, there is a growing library of revealed sources emphasizing the principle to seek learning by study and also by faith.[18] While this subject may be uncomfortable to consider, learning to synthesize secular and spiritual knowledge will leave you a stronger and better person. We strive to harmonize all we can learn to better ourselves and find answers to life's many problems, while not displacing our absolute need for a Savior.

While we will share scriptures, address external influences, and offer quotes from spiritual authorities, nothing we offer should be interpreted as an attack, critique, or evil speaking of sacred things. In addressing this topic in this tone, we have only respect for the scriptures, the Church, and it's membership. The next section is offered as support to Church members and leaders as they seek to understand the intersection of discipleship and this matter of mental health.

The doctrine of Christ and the attendant principles are those teachings that are eternal in their nature, have been and continue to be taught by God's prophets, and pertain to our salvation. There are policies and practices that build on and are an application of that doctrine, but are by their nature changeable and adaptable to fit the needs of the people.

This doctrine of Christ is taught by prophets and apostles. Policies and practices are enacted by the institutional church under the direction of prophets and apostles. However, individuals and groups in the Church can create "folk" doctrines, or hayseed theology, that can end up polluting the teachings that constitute pure doctrine. One consequence of following the counsel of such diluted teachings can be the development of codependent behaviors that appear to be supported by doctrine.

Codependency is a compulsive set of behaviors and characteristics, or in other words, codependency is an addiction. Consequently, codependency is a perversion of the principles of moral agency and of charity. For example, codependent individuals seek to control those who are making certain choices, but they are doing it because they think that is love. This is one area where the plan of salvation can give us guidance. In the premortal existence, the plan of salvation was presented. Lucifer then proposed a major amendment to God's plan that would have been a shift towards extreme codependency—no consequences for our actions. Jehovah's response to the plan was for each of God's children to experience all the consequences for their own actions. Both set forth a pattern that represents the opposing forces of light and dark. Agency without accountability is not agency at all, but a counterfeit.

Saving people from the consequences of their choices is different than helping people who need help. What may appear to be charitable and kind on the surface may also be an expression of codependency.

In the October 2007 general conference, Elder Dallin H. Oaks gave a talk entitled, "Good, Better, Best." The core of this talk was to help differentiate the many degrees of choices that we face daily. He encouraged us to not just do many things that could be considered good, but to determine and act on the b*est* option. This talk has become rooted in the discourse of many Latter-day Saints and has helped establish the notion that our choices and consequences are not all equal. Some have implied that the opposite is also true: there are bad, poor, and worst choices as well (though it doesn't slip off the tongue the same way).

Appraising an individual's choices is an extremely delicate undertaking, if not largely out of mortal purview. However, each individual can develop the gift of divine discernment. Through this gift we weigh the choices with regards to the dictates of moral agency and divine will.

When speaking of codependency in a spiritual or religious context it is absolutely critical to define a middle ground where a choice may appear good but may be done for the wrong reasons. This choice may appear charitable, but it can have a damaging impact on an individual's mental and emotional wellbeing. For the sake of simplicity, we will refer to these choices as "*unhealthy.*"

An act itself may appear or even be quite *good,* if not the b*est.* However, if that act is not chosen freely, or if it assumes responsibility beyond what is laid out by divine decree or policy, it may not qualify as a b*ad, poor, or worst* choice either. "Unhealthy" in this context is not a condemnation but a recognition that there is still a better way to approach certain acts of discipleship.

We don't mean to appear to encourage not being charitable towards one another; in fact, the opposite is the goal. Remember, by its nature, charity must always be an intentional choice—if it is forced or done by compulsion, it is n*ot* charity. The pure love of Christ is always freely given.

Jesus Christ's life, and most poignantly the atoning acts he performed, were a choice—his choice. To classify Jesus Christ as a victim because he took upon himself the pain and suffering for choices he didn't commit assumes that the Atonement was something that was done to him. On the contrary, Jesus Christ willingly submitted to the will of the Father and solidified his place as the central figure in the plan of salvation by choice. The Atonement shows that Jesus Christ understands victimhood, but he cannot rightly be called a victim. Free will and choice are central components of Atonement doctrine, specifically that Jesus Christ had to choose to enter that covenant act. The Atonement didn't "happen to" Jesus. Nor is it the case that he wasn't going to be happy *until* the world repented of their sins.

HOW WOULD YOU EXPLAIN SPIRITUAL
CODEPENDENCY TO SOMEONE ELSE?

Moral Agency and Charity

There are varying definitions of the concept of moral agency. Some assert agency in a very Libertarian view that includes freedom to choose all things with the only negative consequences being the violation of the rights and sovereignty of another. This is more of a temporal concept defining choice and liberty rather than a moral and eternal accountability model. Moral agency can safely be viewed as the God-endowed ability to choose between right and wrong, specifically relating to decisions with moral accountability. Another way of approaching this definition of moral agency would be: choices that lead an individual towards a divine character, or away from it.

Moral agency implies that a power is given to each person to make moral choices. This relies on the assumption that one must have the faculties to process information sufficiently to make an informed decision. "Freedom to choose can be a reality only when we can distinguish between our choices. If we do not know the consequences of our choices, then we cannot know which choice is best. If we do not know the consequences, then we can exercise no more real freedom of choice than someone who is blindfolded and is expected to choose by guessing. Freedom to guess and freedom to choose are not the same thing. Freedom to guess is being given the right to choose while being denied the correct criteria upon which to judge. That is only a pretended freedom. It may look like freedom—we may even accept it as freedom—but in reality it is a kind of slavery instead. When we know and trust God, the Holy Ghost gives us an assurance of the consequences, and therefore actually gives us the freedom to choose."[19]

Moral agency implies some sense of accountability for our choices. Conversely, codependency is a form of control wherein we seek to control the circumstances and consequences of another. Codependent control, specifically the control of the choices and consequences of others, implies a sense of power that is beyond *mortal* ability in some cases, but is beyond *moral* boundaries in all cases.

Moral agency requires that each individual is *responsible for their own choices,* exclusively. Remember that moral agency can only be exercised by those possessing the faculties to make informed decisions. Exclusions include children and others who lack the ability to make moral decisions due to a limited intellectual capacity. In the church we often speak of three distinct categories of accountability: children under age 8 (or people who do not yet possess the mental capacity of an 8-year-old), anyone age 8 or above but who are not yet endowed in the temple, and those who have made temple covenants. Each group experiences an increasing degree of accountability as they progress. As the scripture goes, "For of him unto whom much is given much is required; and he who sins against the greater light shall receive the greater condemnation."[20]

Moral Agency and R*esponsibility or Accountability* are two terms that are inseparably connected in principle. Elder Lynn G. Robbins gave a masterful talk on this subject in a BYU Devotional. I wish to quote a sizable portion here because it is an important step in understanding the relationship of these principles with respect to codependency:

> The Book of Mormon teaches us that we are
> agents to "act . . . and not to be acted upon" (2
> Nephi 2:26)—or to be "free to act for [our]selves"

(2 Nephi 10:23). This freedom of choice was not a gift of partial agency but of complete and total 100 percent agency. It was absolute in the sense that the One Perfect Parent never forces His children. He shows us the way and may even command us, but, "nevertheless, thou mayest choose for thyself, for it is given unto thee" (Moses 3:17).

Assuming responsibility and being accountable for our choices are agency's complementary principles (see Doctrine and Covenants 101:78). Responsibility is to recognize ourselves as being the cause for the effects or results of our choices—good or bad. On the negative side, it is to always own up to the consequences of poor choices.

Except for those held innocent, such as little children and the intellectually disabled, gospel doctrine teaches us that each person is responsible for the use of their agency and "will be punished for their own sins" (Articles of Faith 1:2). It isn't just a heavenly principle but a law of nature—we reap what we sow.

Logically then, complete and total agency comes with complete and total responsibility:

"And now remember, remember, my brethren, that whosoever perisheth, perisheth unto himself; and whosoever doeth iniquity, doeth it unto himself; for behold, ye are free; ye are permitted to act for yourselves; for behold, God hath given unto you a knowledge and he hath made you free." [Helaman 14:30]

One of Satan's most crafty strategies to gain control of our agency isn't a frontal attack on our agency but a sneaky backdoor assault on responsibility. Without responsibility, every good gift from God could be misused for evil purposes. For example, freedom of speech without responsibility can be used to create and protect pornography. The rights of a woman can be twisted to justify an unnecessary abortion. When

the world separates choice from accountability, it
leads to anarchy and a war of wills or survival of the
fittest. We could call agency without responsibility
the Korihor principle, as we read in the book of
Alma "that every man conquered according to his
strength; and whatsoever a man did was no crime"
(Alma 30:17). With negative consequences
removed, you now have agency unbridled, as if
there were no day of reckoning.

An individual experiencing codependency has a complex and often
conflicted relationship with moral agency and responsibility. In a spiritual
or religious sense, an individual can feel a compelling need to save others
who may be caught in sin, trial, or who have some perceived crisis, and
respond to that situation in an overbearing or unhealthy way. This sort of
"ministering" lacks choice, and therefore falls short of being truly
Christlike charity. It may also diminish the blessing of moral agency as it
may deny an individual the consequences of their actions, thereby
reducing the experiential wisdom that comes from it.

To properly minister to one another is to understand that each
person for whom we have an independent relationship is still ultimately
morally responsible for their own actions, and the consequences of those

actions. As such, we should not feel guilty for their choices or undue pressure to make another individual choose differently. There is a limit to our responsibility to help them through whatever trial and situation they may find themselves and to be an influence for good. We can teach, but we cannot coerce. These are the principles upon which the priesthood, God's power, is to operate. "That the rights of the priesthood are inseparably connected with the powers of heaven, and that the powers of heaven cannot be controlled nor handled only upon the principles of righteousness. That they may be conferred upon us, it is true; but when we undertake to cover our sins, or to gratify our pride, our vain ambition, *or to exercise control or dominion or compulsion upon the souls of the children of men,* in any degree of unrighteousness, behold, the heavens withdraw themselves."[21]

One cannot live another's life for them. Nor are we to be responsible for the consequences of their accountable moral actions. Such claims are the exclusive purview of Jesus Christ and his infinite Atonement. While we are to be like our Savior in word and in our hearts, it is both inappropriate to try and impossible to actually be a savior in the exact same way.

Author C.S. Lewis stated, "Of all tyrannies, a tyranny sincerely exercised for the good of its victims may be the most oppressive. It would be better to live under robber barons than under omnipotent moral busybodies. The robber baron's cruelty may sometimes sleep, his cupidity may at some point be satiated; but those who torment us for our own good will torment us without end for they do so with the approval of their own conscience."[22]

HAS THERE EVER BEEN A TIME WHEN YOU PRAYED TO TAKE AWAY SOMEONE'S AGENCY SO THEY WOULD ACT IN A WAY YOU LIKE? HOW WOULD YOU FEEL IF SOMEONE WAS PRAYING TO TAKE AWAY YOUR AGENCY? WHAT DO YOU THINK HEAVENLY FATHER DOES WITH OUR PRAYERS TO TAKE AWAY AGENCY?

"To Act and Not Be Acted Upon"

2 Nephi 2:14-16 is an expansive sermon on the doctrines of creation and the plan of salvation. The creation story is taught so as to give purpose and meaning to the challenges that we face in mortality, but particularly those relating to moral agency. Lehi taught that there are two general categories within God's creation: "God ... hath created all things, both the heavens and the earth, and all things that in them are, both (1) things to act and (2) things to be acted upon" (2 Nephi 2:14; parenthetical added).

God has endowed his children, even from before the creation of this world, with the ability to act. This singular quality is one of the more divine distinctions between God's children and all other creations. The purposes of the plan of salvation and the core reasons for our coming to Earth and experiencing mortality are to act and by doing so learn and gain experiences we would have in no other way. To surrender our core purpose to becoming something that is acted upon is a tragedy of cosmic proportions.

There are many scenarios that show how otherwise good people get scared or desperate and resort to being acted upon. The relationship between family members makes navigating codependent situations an even greater challenge. Identifying who is acting and who is being acted upon can be a powerful and humbling exercise.

Individuals who are codependent or who are experiencing codependency will often feel as if they "have no choice" but to fix other people's problems or clean up after their messes. They treat themselves as beings that are being acted upon. The spouse of an addict may feel they are acted upon every time their addicted spouse indulges in their addiction. The parent of a challenging child may think, "I didn't choose to birth a child with these problems."

A codependent bishop or Relief Society president may feel the burden of a ward member's decision as if they are required to fix every problem that comes to their attention. After all, if someone calls the bishop on the 4th day of the month with their rent due the next day, claiming that they are going to lose their apartment and become homeless if the bishop doesn't cut a check, there may come a sense that the bishop is now somehow responsible for the housing choices of the individual or family. If that bishop doesn't write that check, he may think himself responsible for making a family homeless!

In the scenario just mentioned, no one is really being acted upon. The family or individual who needs rent money likely entered their agreements with their landlord willingly and agreed to terms to pay the rent by a given time. Similarly, the bishop is not the one responsible to pay someone's rent for them. However, scared individuals may push the narrative that the choice to save their family from certain homelessness is in the hands of the bishop. This is a manipulation of the truth.

In efforts to empower individuals to feel a deeper sense of purpose and motivation in this great latter-day work, some have sought to overstate the burdens and responsibilities of discipleship. This can be particularly acute in full-time missionary service.[23] There are stories implying that missionaries hold the keys to someone's salvation based on how valiant ching the gospel. If we aren't working every second of every day in shouting our testimony from the rooftops, the souls of the unconverted will be on our heads. This assertion is a similar misstep to the rent check with the bishop. In reality, salvation is an individual matter. Each person's choices determine their own blessings. While we should choose to express our love for our neighbor by helping where possible (such as in sharing our testimony), we are not responsible for the consequences of that neighbor's choices.

Spiritual codependency occurs, in part, when one feels that they have lost the ability to give, to be charitable by choice. This perceived loss of choice leaves people feeling like victims, like they are being acted upon by others and by "life." The more a person feels victimized by their circumstances or people around them, the less they are able to feel as if they are making a choice to be or do anything, including good things.

In an effort to act and not be acted upon, codependents may overly repair their situation to the point that they seek to control their relationships. This standard promotes a gospel of "results" as opposed to character. This can be a dangerous principle upon which to live one's life. Yet, it is a philosophy forwarded by modern-day motivational speakers all the time. It bases our self-worth on outcomes and not effort, which in turn pushes us to extend beyond the boundaries of agency to compel others so they will obtain the results we desperately need them to achieve. We also believe that without specific results we are worth less than if we had the results for which we intended.

To act or be acted upon is the difference between an agent and a victim.

TO WHAT EXTENT DOES VICTIMHOOD DEFINE YOUR LIFE?

Orthodoxy, Orthopraxy, and Orthopathy

Christian discipleship is the harmonization of three categories: Orthodoxy, orthopraxy, and orthopathy.[24] These three words share the ecclesiastical latin-root "ortho" meaning 'straight or right.' Orthodoxy is learning and believing the 'right truths,' or we might say the true Doctrine of Christ. Orthopraxy is the practicing of those doctrines through the right behaviors, rites, or ordinances—practicing our religion. Orthopathy is orthopraxy for the right reasons, or with the right emotional pieces in place. To Latter-day Saints we may refer to the harmonization of these three concepts as living in "righteousness" - doing the right things for the right reasons or in the right way. We must first seek to obtain the word (orthodoxy)[25], then we must be an example of its teachings (orthopraxy)[26], then we must live the principles in alignment with Jesus Christ's example (orthopathy).

Members of The Church of Jesus Christ of Latter-day Saints are instructed in these matters and encouraged at all levels to live these three principles in harmony. As we increase our orthodoxy, we can also increase in our orthopraxy, and development a more mature orthopathy. Those with codependent tendencies may find themselves struggling with orthopathy, or doing the right things for the right reasons. Orthopathy is a choice that doesn't always come natural when we are overly hung up on determining whether or not our orthopraxy harmonizes with our orthodoxy. As we come to know the Doctrine of Christ, and choose to live its teachings, our nature will progress more and more towards a more complete experience with Christian discipleship.

Can a person be codependent with God?

Can a person be codependent with God? Yes, in a manner of speaking. Codependency is a type of addiction that views people as broken and needing saved, where being the "savior" of others is compulsive and defines part of their character. Most would not view God as broken or in need of salvation. But because a codependent sees someone or something

47

as dependent on them, it is not technically inaccurate to say that an individual can be codependent with religion or even God. While God doesn't need saving, some behave at times as if God or His work will somehow fail without them. Some will find fault with the Church and advocate that they have better ideas on policy. While the Church doesn't always mirror God's ways to perfection, the Church is God's responsibility to lead, not ours. Sometimes people get caught up with this thought because they see themselves acting as God's special agent and, as such, divinely appointed to police others because it shores up their special connection with God. That is the "emotional hit" they seek, even if it isn't the motivation they recognize.

Individuals also run the risk of codependency with God if they feel they have to apologize for God, or they feel that they have to repair the damage they perceive God has inflicted on others. In this case I would extend the definition to include those that feel the need to apologize for damage they perceive as being inflicted by the Church as well. Actual injury or harm doesn't need to take place, just a perception that such has taken place on the part of the codependent.

Alma taught us to "bridle all your passions." Included in that descriptive, "all our passions," is the notion that we can, at times, be out of bounds (or unbridled) with our passion towards God, towards our responsibilities, towards our fellow human beings, and even to ourselves. Religious zeal is a real concern in striving for the balanced life of a disciple of Christ.

Dallin H. Oaks taught, "A related strength that can be corrupted to our downfall is a desire to excel in a Church calling. I remember a graduate student who used his Church service as a means of escape from the rigors of his studies. He went beyond what we call Church-service time and became almost a full-time Church-service worker. He consistently volunteered for every extra assignment, giving help that was greatly appreciated in the various organizations and activities of the Church. As a result of this inordinate allocation of time, he failed in his studies and then mistakenly blamed his failure on the excessive burden of Church service. His strength became his downfall."

Elder Oaks continued: "Similarly, I remember the concerns President Harold B. Lee expressed to me when I was president of BYU. Shortly before the Provo Temple was dedicated, he told me of his concern that the accessibility of the temple would cause some BYU students to attend the temple so often that they would neglect their studies. He urged me to work with the BYU stake presidents to make sure the students understood that even something as sacred and important as temple service needed to be done in wisdom and order so that students would not neglect the studies that should be the major focus of their time during their student years."[27]

To choose discipleship, to not be a slave to a set of behaviors, but to become as our Savior, requires a discipline (hence the word d*isciple)* to live righteous principles in righteousness. This means that we are not just asked to feed and clothe the naked, but that we are to do it because we love them. It also means we are not supposed to starve and be naked in doing so.

Similarly, we ought not read scriptures as some divine homework assignment for which there will be a book report; we read them because we learn of God and feel connected to the spirit of revelation to be in harmony with his purposes. The spirit of consecration is that we willingly engage in exalting choices and develop loving relationships with God and our neighbor. If we are compelled by guilt, if we are over-responsible and overbearing, if we seek to control others into obedience, these are not in harmony with divine character and purpose.

To some, this may feel like constantly analyzing our choices to determine if they are charitable or if they are codependent is unnatural. Fair enough. It should be clear that we are hoping to inform and enable change from a state of being acted upon to a place of acting and choosing discipleship. It is not our intent or hope that we will constantly live in a state of personal analysis and motivational scrutiny. The goal and hope is to remove the compulsion to fix or save others and move towards a more natural expression of love by choice. We feel that this is part of putting off the natural man and becoming a Saint.[28]

We should not feel as if we are a slave to the demands of our faith. Being stuck in the church is not a healthy understanding of the true principles of the gospel of Jesus Christ, or the spirit and motivation behind the programs of The Church of Jesus Christ of Latter-day Saints. Discipleship is the pursuit of our greatest selves; codependency is the diminishing, if not depletion, of one's self. In this light, one of the greatest enemies to greater discipleship is its cunning and deceptively similar counterfeit, codependency.

"Footprints in the Sand" is a widely known story that is presented in four short paragraphs. In the first paragraph, an individual dreams of walking on the beach with the Lord while reviewing the events of their life. In the second, the individual recognizes that at their lowest and darkest points there was only one set of footprints in the sand. Third paragraph, this individual asks why it was when they were in moments of distress there were only one set of footprints, implying that the Lord left them alone when they needed him the most. The final paragraph is the Lord's reply: the footprints in the sand were his because those were the times where he carried the person through the trial. For the codependent, the image might be a single set of footprints because they feel they are the ones who had to carry the Lord.

DOES GOD WANT YOUR OBEDIENCE WITHOUT YOUR HEART ALSO SAYING, "YES"? WHAT DO YOU THINK OF SERVING GOD ONLY OUT OF CODEPENDENCE? IS IT POSSIBLE TO DO THE CORRECT ACTIONS FOR INCORRECT REASONS?

Ministerial Care and Responsibility

There are a number of callings in the church where an individual feels great "weight" as a result of the number of people for whom they have stewardship. Culturally, we speak of bishops, stake presidents, Relief Society presidents, elders quorum presidents, even General Authorities of the church as carrying a heavy mantle with tremendous responsibility. But when it comes down to it, there should be no difference in the *amount* of responsibility they have; what changes is for whom they are responsible to minister.

We speak culturally of the terms *stewardship* and *responsibility* almost interchangeably. According to current Church Correlation standards, the term stewardship should only be used in connection with sacred temple covenants of consecration. But members have a strong tendency to hang on to certain words and use them far beyond their intended use. For the sake of this text, we will try and harmonize with current official terminology and only speak of areas where we have ministerial care or our (institutional) church callings and responsibilities.

Just as a person cannot be held responsible for an area of responsibility for which they have not been assigned, an individual cannot be held responsible for decisions that go beyond the scope of individual moral agency.

For example, an elders quorum president has an administrative responsibility over programs like ministering, temple and family history work, missionary work, and to a limited extent, gospel instruction. Relief Society presidents share in this responsibility. These are areas where they have been given charge to oversee and implement Church programs to the best of their knowledge and ability and as directed by those holding the priesthood keys for that work. These individuals are accountable for the discharge of this duty. But they are not *responsible* for the acts of others outlined by nature of their calling or sphere of responsibility. The ward mission leader may be responsible for holding missionary council meetings, visiting prospective members, and teaching the gospel to investigators and less-active members, but they are not responsible for whether or not the individuals whom they teach accept their teaching.

Another proper example is the Relief Society president, who teaches and encourages members of her unit of the Relief Society to act in all diligence in matters of discipleship and who lives according to those principles herself. She will have no change in her eternal reward based on the faithfulness (or lack thereof) by those for whom she has a responsibility inline with her calling. She is not given a "better spot in heaven" when others choose to be righteous, or a lesser degree of reward when people don't live up to her example and counsel. While serving as Relief Society president she may have a unique set of responsibilities, but the degree to which she is responsible or accountable is the same. She is still only responsible for her own actions.

The President of the Church may have a large sphere of responsibility, but he is no more responsible for the actions of another sentient human being than anyone else. Moral agency requires that an individual can only be found responsible for their own actions. Jesus Christ, through the Atonement, ensured that both justice and mercy would be extended but also that individual responsibility was preserved into the eternities. No one would be held responsible for things for which they had no moral choice. The temple and missionary work on both sides of the veil also helps to preserve and reinforce this concept.

This all relates to codependency because this addiction often develops where an individual feels overly responsible for things that are not in their control. God has defined certain boundaries and limitations on agency when it comes to moral judgment and accountability. While some may define the success of someone's term in a calling based on the righteousness of the people in their sphere of institutional responsibility, this is misplaced adulation. Assuming such is placing excessive responsibility on a calling and the person who holds it. This cultural perception can lead to burnout and serves no holy purpose.

This does not mean that we should not care about the decisions of others, but it does mean that we should not be consumed by them or assume that our worthiness is contingent on the worthiness of others. This can be particularly challenging to parents.[29]

WHAT ARE YOU TRYING TO CONTROL THAT IS ACTUALLY NOT YOURS TO CONTROL? AS A PARENT, DO YOU ALLOW YOUR KIDS TO EXERCISE THEIR AGENCY AND LEARN HARD LESSONS? IN YOUR CALLING DO YOU FEEL RESPONSIBLE FOR THE RESULTS YOUR WORK PRODUCES IN SOMEONE ELSE'S LIFE? DO YOU MINISTER IN A WAY THAT IS TRYING TO MOVE PEOPLE TO A PREDETERMINED OUTCOME?

Unbridled empathy

Empathy, or the acts of understanding, compassion, or even vicariously experiencing the thoughts and feelings of others, has been touted as a high and noble effort. Being empathetic towards others can help others through difficult times and develop a bond between two people who have this shared experience. In many ways, empathy is a Christlike attribute that should be developed.

Unbridled empathy, or empathy that extends beyond experiencing vicariously, is a form of spiritual codependency. Spiritual codependency *can* also be the underlying influence that causes a *few* individuals to become allies, defenders, or propaganda machines in defense of those considered to be marginalized by, or who espouse practices and dogmas that oppose the Church. For these few, it is not enough to empathize with people that experience hardships, they must become victims alongside them or for them. Rather than extend love and compassion to people who are hurting, unbridled empathy can cause individuals to crusade for or even attack others who are the perceived aggressors. In this there is a key difference between being compassionate and empathetic with individuals who experience a variety of trials and supporting destructive paths and practices in the name of loving support.

Love does not require a victim. One does not have to abandon one's own values, opinions, or principles to be empathetic or to love an individual. Empathy does not require that we become the person for whom we are being empathetic. It is in these scenarios where unbridled empathy can develop into full-blown codependency.

Are you feeling tension with the idea of
finding the line between what is codependent
and what is charity? If so, in what ways do
you find yourself trying to justify past
behaviors?

Scrupulosity

"Do you constantly obsess about living the gospel the 'right' way? Do you feel an urgency to repent for the same mistake or sin over and over again because you doubt whether you have repented 'properly'? Do you feel perpetually guilty? If so, you might be struggling with a form of obsessive-compulsive disorder (OCD) known as scrupulosity."[30] While this sounds a bit like a sales pitch for a fictitious product called Scrupulosity, it's not.

Scrupulosity is an intense set of compulsive behaviors defined in part by the persistence and depth of the experience. These behaviors become a sort of attempt to manage or control the anxiety that the individual is experiencing. Similarly, codependency is an attempt to control or manage the chaos and its accompanying anxiety. Both may appear to be compulsive charity or even discipleship. One behavior can lead to the development of the other, but they are distinctly different and are not to be confused.

Scrupulosity turns the individual inward so that their actions are motivated by guilt. Codependency turns the individual's attention outward, and their motivations are a response to the perceived behaviors of others. Both will extend themselves in unhealthy ways that only mimic charity. At times their outward behaviors might mirror one another when it comes to religious or spiritual codependency. One will act to manage internal guilt; the other an overbearing responsibility to fix the errors of others. On the outside, these acts may seem the same, but they have very different motivations and different causes. These conditions must be treated in different ways. Additionally, scrupulosity is a more established disorder with a formal set of protocols for treatment, where codependency is more ambiguous. Psychologist Deborah Theobald McClendon, PhD states:

> Christ can remove our stumbling blocks (see 1
> Nephi 14:1), and through His grace He can
> "make weak things become strong" (Ether 12:27).
>
> But these blessings don't come to us by following
> anxiety's mandates. Scrupulosity masquerades as a

desirable, higher standard of righteousness and personal worthiness—but it's not! Instead, it actually denies Christ and His gospel. Scrupulosity replaces our loving, merciful Father and His Spirit with punishing, crippling anxiety and guilt, creating a rigid, demanding checklist approach to gospel living. This is because scrupulosity isn't about faith; it's about obsessive anxiety.

If you struggle with scrupulosity (or any anxiety that interferes with the quality of your daily life), please seek professional help with a trained and licensed mental health provider. A therapist can help you learn to work through the anxiety in a healthy, adaptive manner so you can learn to avoid succumbing to the obsessive-compulsive cycle. In time, the thoughts will no longer be a trigger to anxiety and inappropriate guilt.

By learning to manage anxiety and focusing on the tenets of pure religion, as outlined here, you can learn to dismiss anxiety's efforts to hijack your religious worship and keep proper perspective on

God's plan of happiness. In so doing, you may be able to once again feel His Spirit without anxiety's distortion and to fully experience the true peace and joy that come from living the gospel."[31]

Scrupulosity is mentioned in this setting because of how it can relate to spiritual codependency. We also want to re-emphasize how important it is to not jump to a diagnosis after a casual encounter or short-term exposure to an individual exhibiting certain symptoms. However, both are treatable and both involve a realignment with their relationship to God and eternal principles. Individuals suffering from these conditions can find hope, but it requires a sometimes painful re-alignment.

―――――

DO YOU SEE ANY SPOTS OF SCRUPULOSITY IN YOUR OWN LIFE? DO YOU SUSPECT THAT IT MIGHT BE A GOOD IDEA TO TALK TO A PROFESSIONAL ABOUT IT? WHAT DO YOU THINK HEAVENLY FATHER WOULD SAY TO THE PERSON STRUGGLING WITH SCRUPULOSITY?

―――――

Summary of Codependent Discipleship or Spiritual Codependency

For members of The Church of Jesus Christ of Latter-day Saints, we can feel, quite accurately at times, a driving commitment towards the salvation of souls. We celebrate such commitment and the freedom that living the gospel of Jesus Christ promises. So when we speak of spiritual codependency, we don't wish to call good evil or state that these desires are wrong. However, it is important to strive to find the balance in life that allows us to act and not be acted upon and to give of ourselves freely. God's grace frees us to be as He is; it does not bind us to a set of obligatory or overbearing assignments. Spiritual codependency is a perversion of God's right ways and is perhaps more common than we may have previously considered.

In summary, Spiritual codependency could be defined as: *A set of persistent behaviors where an individual feels compelled to be over responsible for the salvation, or spiritual and emotional well-being, of those with whom they have a formal or implied responsibility, or where behaviors are impacted negatively by the immoral use of agency by others.*

CHAPTER 3 – OVERCOMING AND LEARNING NEW WAYS

"LIFE WITH GOD IS NOT IMMUNITY FROM DIFFICULTIES, BUT PEACE IN DIFFICULTIES."

C. S. Lewis

————◆————

To the codependent we may ask, "Who is the god whom you serve? Is it the Living God, Jesus Christ our Lord, who loves and empowers us? Or is your service to satisfy an anxious compulsion, or even to reduce the disorder and damage you perceive as fostered by the actions of another? Do you spend your life reducing the agency of others to reduce the damage or remove the consequences you see them cause? Do you feel that some of your choices are the corruption of pure and virtuous principles in that they promise peace but leave you feeling tired and used?"

These may be incredibly painful realizations to come to and may cause some anxiety in themselves. Some may even begin to worry about the amount of stress and pain that codependency may have caused others to feel. There may be a heavy and overwhelming weight that the very thing you abhor in others may be the thing you have caused to take place. While there is no way to eliminate the pain of the past, you have the ability to reduce its presence in the future.

Identifying the many ways in which codependency can manifest itself is one half of addressing the issue. In some cases, codependency becomes a weed that slowly takes over your lawn until it becomes your lawn. We may be surprised how long it takes to fully restore what once was and in how many ways that weed will try to spring back up in daily life. A notable shift must take place in order to restore an individual to a sense of order. But even with that shift, it doesn't mean we will never have little "moments" that pop up and annoy.

Overcoming any addictive or compulsive behavior brings a variety of challenges to manage. For some the change will feel like they have to remove many parts of what they see as their core identity. While this is not necessarily the case, that doesn't change the internal experience of the person feeling the challenges. This process can be quite scary, even painful at times, but that is what happens with compulsive behaviors. Codependency is a parasitic condition that can suck the life out of otherwise charitable people.

Recovery, at times, doesn't just feel like we are metaphorically exercising to reduce some fat on our body; it can feel like we are performing complex surgery to remove infected limbs. We feel as if these compulsive behaviors are "part of who we are." Even though we can see how addictive behavior can degrade us, we don't like to see ourselves as broken. Even acknowledging that we have a problem can be overwhelming at times. Addictions can be like an old friend, even if they are an abusive and unwanted leech that only loves us as long as they need us. As painful as it can be, consider your relationship to such individuals and seek ways to establish healthy boundaries.

Like other challenges of our mortal experience, overcoming our natural or fallen conditions, like codependency, may require the grace of God. In fact, we highly recommend God's grace to be a welcomed addition in all of life's experiences. Jesus Christ, through the acts of Atonement, has shown us the way to restore order from chaos, to bring light where there is darkness, and bring life-giving water to the parched lips of the wanderer. As painful and as trapped as an individual may feel in these situations, the power of the Almighty is sufficient to guide individuals and health care professionals through the quagmire of recovery.

Alma, the reformed rebel turned prophet, once asked, "And now behold, I ask of you, my brethren of the church, have ye spiritually been born of God? Have ye received his image in your countenances? Have ye experienced this mighty change in your hearts? Do ye exercise faith in the redemption of him who created you? Do you look forward with an eye of faith, and view this mortal body raised in immortality, and this corruption raised in incorruption, to stand before God to be judged according to the deeds which have been done in the mortal body?"[32] Alma is asking if we have been converted to the gospel of Jesus Christ, and as such are we able to see life with a new paradigm? How about you? Are you seeing life differently after coming to some understanding of codependency? Are you ready to see life in a new way, through a new lens?

Recovery provides a new lens through which we see the scriptures. Recovery has brought new meaning to the scripture from Alma 5, quoted above, specifically the phrase "corruption raised in incorruption." His principle can be seen with a new meaning in light of mental health issues. How potent a descriptor is the word *corruption* when speaking of the complexity of compulsive behaviors. Indeed, the Light of Christ has brought many from the corruption of addiction to the incorruption of true and lasting recovery.

Lived experience can weave a web of snares that can act as triggers for so many mental health behaviors. To overcome these issues, it may not be as easy as simply taking down that web or doing a little house cleaning. We can't vacuum up emotional trauma and have it be "fixed." The brain is a complex and beautiful part of our divine creation. But this fallen world can do a number on our minds depending on what makes up our environment and history. Time and patience are needed to trust in the healing process and in the Healer of our souls. It may appear that it took "a day" to bring order from chaos during the Genesis creation accounts, but our own healing may require weeks, months, or even years.

Christ-Centered Healing

Experiencing Codependency involves developing unhealthy views of ourselves and our relationships. The best and most lasting way to experience healing from codependency is in and through Jesus Christ. He sees us with perfect eyes, and with a universal and eternal love. He not only knows us, but he knows the people with whom we have developed a codependent relationship. His everlasting love and all-knowing perspective is something in which we can trust. This trust should allow us to let go, to not seek to fix or control others. How we seek to treat others can be seen as a sign of our faith in Christ. Do we trust Christ to shepherd them? Do we trust Christ to shepherd us? Is seeking to fix and control others and their consequences in opposition to that trust?

Part of Christ-centered healing is re-evaluating ourselves, and seeing those with whom we have a relationship with new eyes. Sister

Michelle D. Craig said, "Perhaps the most important things for us to see clearly are who God is and who we really are—sons and daughters of heavenly parents, with a "divine nature and eternal destiny." Ask God to reveal these truths to you, along with how He feels about you. The more you understand your true identity and purpose, soul deep, the more it will influence everything in your life."

Codependency views ourselves as a fixer, and to a certain extent the victim of others. Codependency also views others as hopelessly broken. But is this how God views us? Sister Craig continues, "Understanding how God sees us prepares the way to help us see others as He does. Jesus Christ sees people deeply. He sees individuals, their needs, and who they can become. Where others saw fishermen, sinners, or publicans, Jesus saw disciples; where others saw a man possessed by devils, Jesus looked past the outward distress, acknowledged the man, and healed him."

Viewing others the way Christ views us takes time and prayer. With prayer will be invited to repent and see the situations and the people, differently. Sister Craig also advised, "As I pray for the Lord to open my eyes to see things I might not normally see, I often ask myself two questions and pay attention to the impressions that come: "What am I doing that I should stop doing?" and "What am I not doing that I should start doing?" If we treat others codependently, what am I doing that I should stop doing, and what am I doing that I should start doing? What changes when we view ourselves and others the way Christ sees us?

The answer to codependency is not inaction or indifference. To be a disciple of Jesus Christ still requires us to care deeply, to view and encourage the divine potential in others, but also to view them as children of a loving God in whom we can trust to guide their lives. Sister Craig offers this encouragement, "As with all gifts the Father so willingly offers, seeing deeply requires us to a*sk Him*—and then a*ct*. A*sk* to see others as He does—as His true sons and daughters with infinite and divine potential. Then a*ct* by loving, serving, and affirming their worth and potential as prompted. As this becomes the pattern of our lives, we will find ourselves becoming "true followers of ... Jesus Christ." Others will be able to trust our hearts with theirs. And in this pattern we will also discover o*ur own t*rue identity and purpose. Through His grace, He will bless us and increase our capacity. Through the power of the Holy Ghost, Christ will enable us to s*ee* ourselves and s*ee* others as He does. With His help, we can discern what is most needful. We can begin to see the hand of the Lord working in and through the ordinary details of our lives—we will see deeply."

To overcome codependency, we must be willing to allow God to change our countenances so we can see things with new eyes—to see deeply as Sister Craig has counseled. When reading the scriptures and the words of prophets and apostles with these new eyes, we may find that God has been planting the seeds of hope all along the way. All it takes is us giving those seeds a place to fulfill the measure of their creation. We, the authors of this book, stand as witnesses that God is the Healer of our hearts, mights, minds, and souls. We can say with some sense of personal experience that overcoming codependency and many other mental health issues is possible. God can bring order to the chaos, wisdom where there is doubt, and guidance through the mists of darkness towards the brilliant Tree of Life.

IN WHAT WAYS SHOULD JESUS CHRIST PLAY IN OVERCOMING CODEPENDENCY?

Jesus is our perfect picture of a non-codependent person. He saw need all around him, but he did not heal everyone just because they demanded it of him. He did not answer every single question that was asked of him very clearly. He interacted with the individuals of his day on his own terms, not theirs. He knew when people were trying to trap and manipulate him. He knew that he would heal some and they would not show gratitude. But he did it anyway - not because they earned it but because he chose to do so.

Sometimes we have this picture of Jesus being a 1st century teacher who wanders around and just tends to whatever is in front of him in a haphazzard way. It's not true. Instead Jesus made choices about who to converse with. Who to heal. Who to spar with. His choices were driven by his agenda to do the things the Father sent him to do.

DO YOU EVER FEEL LIKE "BEING MORE LIKE JESUS"
MEANS BEING MORE CODEPENDENT? IN WHAT WAYS
DO YOU SEE HIM AS RESISTING CODEPENDENCY?

Wisdom and Order

Elder Neal A. Maxwell wrote an article published in the June 1994 *Ensign* entitled "Wisdom and Order." This article could be considered apostolic counsel on the issue of what is secularly referred to as codependency. Elder Maxwell starts out,

> As precious and special assets of the Lord's kingdom,
> Latter-day Saints must recognize the wisdom of
> preserving their health and strength in order to serve

more individuals and to serve them longer. "People fatigue" can overtake us all if we are not wise.

Many persons, in dealing with the pressures of life, have developed their own ways of handling stress and "people fatigue." I offer some confirmation and encouragement for them to continue pacing themselves. Those who have worked out things reasonably well likely are aligned with scriptural counsel....

Each of us has different strengths and faces different circumstances that call for calibrations that are highly individual. Happily, the Lord really does increase the capacity of the diligent, as He surely did in the case of Joseph Smith and Eliza Snow....

Many things in life act upon us over which we have no control, but there is a zone—of differing size for each of us—in which we can act for ourselves, rather than merely be acted upon (see 2 Ne. 2:26)....

Basic scriptures can guide us as we seek to manage ourselves wisely. As King Benjamin counseled, "See that all these things are done in wisdom and order; for it is not requisite that a man should run faster than he has strength" (Mosiah 4:27)....

A revelation was given to the Prophet Joseph Smith at a time when he must have been exceedingly anxious to finish the important and urgent translation of the Book of Mormon:

"Do not run faster or labor more than you have strength and means provided to enable you to translate; but be diligent unto the end" (Doctrine and Covenants 10:4)....

Thus, the Lord has given us what might be called the "wisdom and order" and "strength and means" tests. Unwisely, we often write checks against our time accounts as we never would dare do, comparably, against our bank accounts. Sometimes we make so many commitments that they become like the vines in the allegory of Jacob, threatening to "overcome the roots," including the "roots" of family relationships, friendships, and relationships with God....

On my office wall is a quote from Anne Morrow Lindbergh: "My life cannot implement in action the demands of all the people to whom my heart responds."

For those overwhelmed with the many ways in which you see a growing need to fix the world around you, we have apostolic and divine permission to invoke the power of "no." Sometimes we need to say "no" to things, some of which are truly good things. This is an issue that affects many people, not just members of the Restored Church, but it does seem that there are many scriptures that speak to the need for balance and avoid "burn out" within the Latter-day Saint scriptural canon. Elder Maxwell continued:

> The original Twelve were counseled that they were not to "serve tables" (see Acts 6:1–4). Actually, serving tables is easy. It is visible, measurable, and do-able—compared to opening up the nations of the world to missionary work or to keeping wolves out of the flock. But if the Twelve were drawn away from their scriptural and constitutional duties, the whole Church would suffer. Being drawn away can happen to all of us, almost without our knowing it."
>
> "Wisdom and order" recognize that there are seasons in life for certain extra chores. Professional responsibilities and formal callings come and go, but it is always in season to follow Jesus' commandment:

"What manner of men [and women] ought ye to be?

Verily I say unto you, even as I am" (3 Ne. 27:27).

One of the many challenges along the path of the disciples' journey is finding balance. Being dedicated but not over-dedicated to the point of burnout and finding time for serving others while not neglecting ourselves can be difficult.

Elder Maxwell continued:

> The Lord knows we "cannot bear all things now" (Doctrine and Covenants 50:40). However, His grace is sufficient for us for each of life's seasons, if we are humble (see Ether 12:27).
>
> Wisdom and order help us cope with "people fatigue" and commitments beyond our strength and means. Wisdom and order prompt us to "sit a spell" with loved ones and colleagues, allowing us time for life's extra chores, and remind us that we cannot bear all things now.
>
> The demands and challenges of our day are great, but wisdom and order help us maintain our

perspective. That perspective, in turn, allows us to do all things in "wisdom and order," that thereby we might "win the prize" (Mosiah 4:27), even exaltation and eternal life with those we have loved and with those we have served.

Running Faster Than We Have Strength

In the Book of Mormon, King Benjamin powerfully taught his people the principles, patterns, and call for balance in the quest for Christian discipleship. Near the end of that sermon, King Benjamin taught what I would call the linchpin that holds together the practical elements of the gospel of Jesus Christ in a healthy, empowering, and exalting way. After illuminating the path through repentance, which is the path of change towards a more righteous life, King Benjamin declared, "And now, for the sake of these things which I have spoken unto you—that is, for the sake of retaining a remission of your sins from day to day, that ye may walk guiltless before God—I would that ye should impart of your substance to the poor, every man according to that which he hath, such as feeding the hungry, clothing the naked, visiting the sick and administering to their relief, both spiritually and temporally, according to their wants. And see that all these things are done in wisdom and order; for it is not requisite that a man should run faster than he has strength. And again, it is expedient that he should be diligent, that thereby he might win the prize; therefore, all things must be done in order."[33]

The balance of *wise* effort and the demands of *order* can be challenging to achieve. We seem to live in a world that is not short on options of what to do with our time or tragedies with people that need rescuing. With so many potential sources that place a demand on our limited resources, many individuals don't seem to have a problem with committing to help others in general but rather in choosing precisely what to commit to. There comes a point in the path of discipleship where our principles are tested and our relationships are put under a microscope—we are given information upon which we can act, or we can be acted upon. We prioritize in both healthy and unhealthy ways. Some learn from this process and enact constructive behaviors, while others can become a slave to their choices and commitments.

When our spiritual and emotional immune systems are taxed, just like our bodies, a reaction takes place. For some, this reaction can be to shut down, to retreat, to be "inactive." Others may go into overdrive, feeling that greater dedication breeds greater control, and where there is control there is harmony. Where this latter scenario is present, behaviors can easily transform into "running faster than we have strength." In taking either of these directions—inactivity or hyperactivity—we encounter the principle of codependency. While codependency feels like a defense or coping mechanism, it is largely unsustainable—it is not eternal.

Individuals can emotionally lift more than they can carry; however, they may then feel guilty when they have to stop "helping others who need the help more than they do." Others see themselves as a burden to others during a period while they are themselves broken. Either form is letting guilt take charge, which never leads to rest of the conscience.

So how does recovery take place? Where do we find best practices in these areas? We reiterate, there is no substitute for the divine hand of God holding hands with the care of trusted medical and mental health professionals. However, we also want to introduce to you concepts that will help to start the healing process and the reprocessing effort, some sources that have been helpful in recovery from codependency.

Self-Care

Let's start with an area that has long been neglected for the codependent: one's self. "Self-care" is a concept that can sound selfish, self-absorbed, and in some ways in opposition to the scripture, "He who finds his life will lose it, and he who loses his life for my sake will find it."[34] For the codependent this is particularly scary. If they are not 100% dedicated to managing everyone else, things will fall apart, creating an even bigger mess for them to clean up. Even 5% of time in self-care means it will take 105% effort to make up for that time. Codependents are so obsessed with the world around them that the idea of shutting out the outside world for even a half hour can be an anxiety-inducing prospect.

The concept of self-care for Latter-day Saints is fully in harmony with the principles of our faith. In fact, one could make the argument that the plan of salvation is a macro application of true and balanced self-care. We improve ourselves while helping to encourage others to improve as well. The work of God is to bring about the salvation of man and the exaltation of our souls. This effort requires that each individual improve and grow. In doing so, we also increase our capacity to do good in the world. As we care for others, feed the hungry, and clothe the naked, we should be growing in our capacity to love and be like Christ. These are not mutually exclusive ideas; they must go hand in hand. If we never care for ourselves and neglect increasing our own lives, our fallen condition will get the better of us and leave us unable to fill the measure of our creation.

Christian theologian Dietrich Bonhoeffer developed a fascinating notion that we should not be engaged in selfless giving but rather in something that amounts to self-full giving, for this promotes the notion that the more fully developed we are personally the more we are in a position to help others. Selfless giving, on the other hand, eventually deteriorates our ability to help others. Christ, being a fully developed individual, possessing all good attributes to perfection, is in the best position to provide help to all, thus enabling divine self-full giving.

IS "BURNING OUT" TRYING TO FIX THE SINS AND TRANSGRESSIONS OF OTHERS "GIVING OF YOUR BEST SELF?"

To more fully develop oneself, we must first address who we are and how we are "designed." There are four quadrants or aspects to our lives: Mental, Physical, Spiritual, and Emotional. Time and care must be given to increase our capacities in each of these four aspects or we will be unbalanced and eventually unmanageable. For some codependents, even reading this book will feel so selfish that they may not want to keep reading for fear some situation will need them and they won't be there to fix or save it. But, reading this book can help address the mental, spiritual, and emotional care that one is needing. (Attach some weights to your wrists as you read, and it can help address some physical care as well!)

Being charitable requires the ability "to do." Without self-care, one's ability "to do" things charitably (because we are under so much stress and strain) will fall short of what we are asked "to be" as disciples of Christ. Thus, the first area of change for the codependent is to come to the understanding that each individual is expected to take time for self-care. It is as Elder Maxwell counseled, "Unwisely, we often write checks against our time accounts as we never would dare do, comparably, against our bank accounts. Sometimes we make so many commitments that they become like the vines in the allegory of Jacob, threatening to 'overcome the roots,' including the 'roots' of family relationships, friendships, and relationships with God."[35]

Just as you can overwater a plant, you can saturate yourself in acts you deem as charitable to the point that you drown. Don't underestimate the power of something as simple as taking a deep breath, closing your eyes, and saying a genuine prayer for help, strength, and guidance. Prayer is one of the simplest forms of self-care. If you are too busy to pray, you are too busy.

HOW ARE YOU CARING FOR YOURSELF IN EACH
AREA OF LIFE - MENTAL? PHYSICAL? SPIRITUAL?
EMOTIONAL? ARE YOU EVER TEMPTED TO GIVE
MORE THAN YOU HAVE? WHAT IS YOUR REACTION
WHEN YOU GET OVERWHELMED - WHAT ROLE DOES
PRAYER PLAY IN THAT? HOW CAN YOU BETTER USE
PRAYER AS AN ACT OF SELF CARE?

Reframing Love

Overcoming codependency may require reframing how we look at love. In some ways a codependent may see their actions as kindness, and "bear(ing) one another's burdens, that they may be light."[36] However, if we are preventing individuals from their own progression, or if our actions are enabling spiritual atrophy, our actions may be causing undue harm. These actions may also involve denying individuals the lessons that a mortal life was designed to give. Coming to the understanding that who you are and the choices you have made for years (maybe even decades) doesn't quite fit the definition of charity/love, may leave a codependent feeling lost, confused, perhaps even guilty. What can be even more troubling moving forward is the constant second guessing--is what I am doing an act of love, or is it continuing the pattern of self-preserving codependency?

In a recent sacrament meeting, a speaker offered an insight that can help exemplify the fallacy that codependency is love. Imagine a person laying on a weight bench at the gym while their trainer stands above them, lifting the weights for them. Who is getting the benefit of the workout? The person laying on the bench has less exertion and therefore less 'stress or pain' commonly associated with working out; but they also receive no benefit for simply laying there. The trainer doing all the workouts for their multiple clients throughout the day might find that they can't keep doing everyone's workouts for them. The trainer will tire of exhaustion, and the clients will eventually quit as they will find no positive results from their 'workout.' In this way, neither the trainer or the client are edified for their effort.

For so long codependents have convinced themselves that what they were doing was for the good of the person whom they were overly responsible. They lift the weights so that other people wouldn't have to— they are a trainer. Isn't that what trainers do? So much of a codependent's life is defined by how they help/fix/control others that changing that may seem like a complete personality overhaul. Some have operated with a certain view of themselves that they may ask, "If what I was doing wasn't love, then what is love?" The codependent that chooses to overcome their addiction is faced with a very painful reorganizing of their life, their motivations, and who they are to their core.

Perfect—Now!?!

In every conceivable way, God is the goal. God's existence is the ideal standard that can intimidate some and inspire others. For some, the lofty standards of celestial living is inspiring and guides one to a meaningful existence. Others struggle to even desire to live up to the "ideal" due to the gaping chasm that lies between them and their potential. The ideal is a complete and whole existence—perfection forever can be intimidating.

The "ideal" is a daunting if not impossible goal in mortality. Yet we still teach and speak of the ideal, and we encourage full gospel living. The only way to achieve perfection is to strive for it continually. Perfection is no accident or unintentional result—perfection must be chosen. When it comes to our mortal experience we may learn of perfection and celestial ideals, but then we impose an arbitrary deadline for their realization. Elder Jeffrey R. Holland counseled, "May I remind all of us that we live in a fallen world and for now we are a fallen people. We are in the telestial kingdom.

As President Russell M. Nelson has taught, here in mortality perfection is still 'pending.'"[37]

Eternal progression is one of the promised blessings for the righteous. Therefore it would be irrational to assume that even in the post-mortal world we would be granted instant perfection. We have an eternity to experience, to grow, and to learn how to best fulfill these ideals, and, as Elder Holland taught, to "Be Ye Therefore Perfect—Eventually."[38]

So, when speaking of the ideals of human behavior, there can be no time clock to impose, nor does our spiritual existence begin at birth nor at the end of mortality. Mortal life is not a championship sporting event with a final buzzer at the time of death signaling those who "win" and those who "lose." This means that not only are the people around us going to continue to be imperfect, it also means that each codependent will be imperfect for some time after this mortal probation. This level of imperfection is not a surprise to God; in fact, he created a whole world in which we would experience imperfection with the goal of learning from it. Our imperfections are something to learn from, not a thing to fix in others. Just as the scriptures say, "And why beholdest thou the mote that is in thy brother's eye, but considerest not the beam that is in thine own eye?"[39]

The goal of our imperfections is to lead us to see things clearly, not simply for the exercise of identifying motes and beams.

So, take a deep breath, and do what you can to erase the expectation of being perfect in this life. No amount of stress on our part will perfect those around us, and no amount of our exercising control over them will bring them to perfection either. Perfection is not in our power alone, nor is it congruent with the plan of salvation for us to rely on anyone other than the Savior for that to take place.

HOW FRUSTRATED DO YOU GET WITH YOURSELF WHEN YOU NOTICE THAT YOU ARE NOT PERFECT? HOW FRUSTRATED DO YOU GET AT OTHER PEOPLE WHEN YOU SEE THAT THEY'RE NOT TRYING HARD ENOUGH? DOES HAVING AN ETERNAL PERSPECTIVE HELP? WHAT IS IT LIKE FOR YOU WHEN YOU TRY TO CONTROL PEOPLE INTO ACTING PERFECT?

Overcoming Codependency

As each codependency scenario is unique, so will be each recovery experience. In some scenarios the remedies may take extended periods to enact. In others that change may come sooner than later. Some may find help from their bishop or Relief Society president, while others might find help from their ministering brother or sister, maybe even a family member.

But in the end, the answers or solutions for codependency must also come from within. One must be capable of initiating and choosing change for this restoration to take place in a meaningful way. Regardless of the struggle required, the battle for self-mastery is a worthy endeavor with eternally rewarding consequences.

Influence, impact, encouragement—these are the hallmarks of discipleship as they are the hallmarks of a God who gifted and eternally honors moral agency. Compulsion, coercion, fear—these are the defining tactics of the adversary.

Chapter 4 - Theories or Helpful Approaches

"The greatest discovery in life is self-discovery.
Until you find yourself you will always be
someone else. Become yourself."

Myles Munroe

——————— ◆ ———————

[Note: Most chapters in this book are written by Nick and Jennifer together. But there are some exceptions. In this chapter Jennifer is the primary writer due to her background as a mental health professional. These sources are not from Latter-day Saint authors, nor are they faith based. However, codependency does not have a large corpus of sources from spiritual or religious context. With some discipline, these sources can be read with a spiritual lens.]

There are many different ways to approach treating codependency. Just as headaches and body pain can be managed with different types of pills, treatments, or approaches, treatments for codependency also come in different forms and must be adapted and implemented with the care of mental health professionals. It would be wonderful if there was some "pill" that one could take. If that were possible, more than a few people would invest in such an idea. Until the miracle pill is created, there are effective (non-pharmaceutical) approaches, as well as informational and explanatory texts that can be powerful in their application.

Historically one might look to *Codependent No More* by Melody Beattie as a resource. That book started off what would be decades worth of research into treatments. Since that book was written, treatments have been developed that date that text and place it in the category of "informational" as opposed to therapeutically necessary.

Originally published in 1986, *Codependent No More* is the classic text on codependency. This book introduced millions to the concept, and it has been translated into dozens of languages. It remains a best seller for good reason. If you want to understand the earliest discussions of codependency, it is a great source, though we offer a few caveats: (1) It is not written specifically with faith or church issues in mind. (2) Our understanding of codependency has developed since 1986. Some of the ways this book presents things might be said quite differently if it were being written today. What the author presents was only generally conceptualized back in 1986. However, that text served as a catalyst for this area of study. As a result of *Codependent No More,* much has been developed, and treatment options have become more robust and empirically validated.

While it was written from a secular point of view, the text recognized that codependent people have fallen into the trap of being acted upon instead of choosing their own actions. "Codependents are reactionaries. They overreact. They under-react. But rarely do they act. They react to the problems, pains, lives, and behaviors of others."[40]

Beattie's solution is straightforward. The codependent person must (1) gain awareness about the issue, (2) come to understand why they feel compelled to solve the other person's problem, and (3) learn to relate with empathy to other people's problems without having to take responsibility for the problem.

This simple summary of these three steps is easier said than done and doesn't necessarily address the nuances of the individual circumstances of each codependent. Some people are able to follow this process on their own and be quite successful, but many are not. Gaining insight into why one feels compelled to solve another person's problems is hard work, and our ability for self-deception is great. Consultation with a therapist (who can also be called a counselor, mental health counselor, psychologist, or many other titles) can help.

Effective Approaches

A variety of approaches to treating codependency have emerged in the last two decades. While each of them has a slightly different focus, all of them have the goal of helping the person who suffers from codependency to live a life of love and freedom. Sometimes people who suffer from codependency fear making changes to their style of relating because the bonds of codependent relating are strong—and while they might not be healthy, they are better than no bonds at all. People suffer for longer than needed because of this. Therapists hear clients say things like, "If I put up a boundary, they will leave me. I'd rather have poor boundaries and still be able to get SOME love, than have great boundaries and get no love." And this is understandable. But it doesn't have to be this way. The goal of treating codependency is not so you end up less happy in your relationships but rather so you can have more genuine connection, more genuine love.

In the following section we will offer a sample of approaches for how to heal from codependency. This is not a comprehensive overview of all possible treatments for codependency, nor is it even a recommendation for which approach is right for you. These are starting points in exploring your relationship to codependency. We also hope that you will understand that healing is possible. You might even recognize one of these approaches as resonating with how healing could happen for you.

Loving What Is by Byron Katie

The book, "Loving What Is" has become an unlikely source for addressing the topic of Codependency. While it is not based on a particular therapeutic model, nor does it claim to address codependency specifically, it is quite practical when it comes to short-circuiting the mental pathways and behaviors of people who show Codependent tendencies. Codependents, like many in some form of compulsive behavior, have a tendency to view the world in a way that most comfortably justifies their behaviors. This defense mechanism can be summed up with the adage, 'we are very good at believing our own press releases.' It is important to develop the ability to disconnect with the false reality we have tried to construct for so long. That is a process that takes time. This is

kes time to develop these patterns in the first place,
lue them.

In the book, "Loving What Is," Byron Katie establishes a practical
approach that she calls "The Work." "The Work is simply four questions
that, when applied to a specific problem, enable you to see what is
troubling you in an entirely different light. As Katie says, "It's not the
problem that causes our suffering, it's our thinking about the problem."[41]
Additionally, this book helps to establish the three kinds of 'business' in
the universe; mine, your's, and God's. Katie states, "Much of our stress
comes from mentally living out of our own business. When I think, 'You
need to get a job, I want you to be happy, you should be on time, you need
to take better care of yourself,' I am in your business. When I am worried
about earthquakes, floods, war, or when I will die, I am in God's business.
If I am mentally in your business or in God's business, the effect is
separation. If you are living your life and I am mentally living your life, who
is here living mine? We're both over there. Being mentality in your
business keeps me from being present in my own. I am separate from
myself, wondering why life doesn't work."[42]

Taking this concept further, the idea that we are living in the other's
space seems to imply that we don't love who they are, and that we think we
know better and can fix them. This is another manifestation of how some

can become Codependent towards God, because they are in God's business as if they have power to control it, or that they know better how to do 'god' than God does. To be in someone else's business is not love, it is arrogance. To truly come to 'love what is' rather than be wrapped up in expectations for other people, is actually quite liberating. You can learn to love people where they are at rather than judge them for falling short of our expectations. The challenge is learning how to be in our own 'business' while still making space for empathy.

While this approach may seem selfish or incongruous with Latter-day Saint teachings on charity to some, I assure you that the text is actually empowering and is largely a safe resource. It teaches to truly learn to love without needing to fix or change people. This is not to say we can't invite people to change, repent, or come unto Christ-we always should. But we don't see that repentance as a prerequisite for love and understanding. There is no set of behaviors that we need to have in place before we can treat each other with love. We love people who repent and we love people who don't repent. This is divine love, this is God's love, this is Charity. To invite, not mandate, is freedom and it is empowering in the relationships we foster with God or His Children. To love universally is to see our own value and strength, while seeing the value and strength in others.

The basics of "The Work" is this, 1) identifying the thought behind the suffering, 2) do "The Work" to reprocess those thoughts. While "The Work" is categorized as 4 questions you ask yourself, there is clearly more to it than just these four questions. When one encounters a stressful thought, or in this context, when a codependent is being triggered to fix or be responsible for someone else's business, you ask yourself the "four" questions. The four questions are:

1. **Is it true?** - Meaning, is the thought that you are experiencing true, or is it just something made up or reactionary?

2. **Can you absolutely know that it is true?** - This may seem like a silly bit of redundancy, but if you are being true to yourself, this is a helpful step.

3. **How do you react, what happens, when you believe that thought?** - Meaning, how do you feel inside, and how do you treat a person when you have this stressful thought towards them?

4. **Who would you be without that thought?** -This is a sobering exploration for the codependent. So much of a codependent identity is wrapped up in these stress-inducing thoughts. To part with these thoughts is enlightening but painful--and necessary to recovery.

These four questions are followed by additional exercises that are best served by reading and applying the original text. There is also a sort of phantom question, question 3b if you will, that is important to point out. This can be the most powerful way to d0 a self-examination on this subject, "Can you find one *stress-free* reason to keep that thought?" If one is to walk through the process called "The Work" and ask these questions about the areas where they intersect with codependency, and if you do this honestly, it will change you in powerful ways.

"Loving What Is" helps to short circuit that thinking and allows the individual to be more open to love, and less inclined for resentment and bitterness. It helps to stem the tide of self deception, and helps each person to have a greater understanding of reality; thus empowering them to live with greater peace and purpose. Ultimately, this text will challenge you to see if you can give yourself the medicine you have dispensing for years.

DBT

"Dialectical Behavior Therapy (DBT) is a cognitive-behavioral treatment developed by Marsha Linehan, Ph.D., in the 1980s to treat people with borderline personality disorder (BPD). Those diagnosed with

BPD often experience extremely intense negative emotions that are difficult to manage. These intense and seemingly uncontrollable negative emotions are often experienced when the individual is interacting with others—friends, romantic partners, family members."[43] Similarly, codependency involves deep emotions that inform toxic decisions that arise from certain relationships. These emotions are difficult to manage, which negatively impacts those relationships as a result.

Since the 1980s, DBT has been shown effective in treating a number of behavior conditions. The premise of DBT is that healthy people can hold two different points of view. Both can be true, even though they seem at odds, yet the person can find consonance in the duality of that experience. The D in DBT refers to dialectics—finding the balance in opposites. Another way of viewing this is finding the truth that rests in harmonizing points of view that may seem to conflict with the other.

A healthy person can accept themselves non-judgmentally in whatever situation they find themselves and also work toward making their situation better. For example, a person who is struggling because they want to micromanage their adult child's job search can recognize the situation in which they find themselves (*"My son's resume is so bad, I have a really strong impulse to fix it for him so that he can get a job"*) and not judge themselves negatively for it. They can then convert that inner dialogue to simple recognition of this impulse, "Here I am wishing I could take responsibility for fixing all my son's problems. This desire comes up in me from time to time, and now I'm noticing it's here again."

The key here is to choose to do something different than a codependent impulse, which is to take over and fix things. DBT helps individuals come to the answer while recognizing the various extremes that can be present in their own minds. DBT trains the mind to respond this way, "I'm going to keep my mouth closed on this subject and wait to see if my help is asked for. If they don't ask for my help, then I may offer support. If they do not accept the offering, then I won't act hurt but will accept their 'no' with grace and support him in other ways that are welcome."

Getting from entertaining a codependent impulse to fix things to accepting the other person's "no" and acting with grace takes a lot of work. DBT teaches and facilitates the practice of the skills to address these impulses in safe settings. It also helps to coach our minds to be less concerned with the negative outcomes and to trust others in the present. Like the text *Loving What Is*, DBT focuses on principles of mindfulness, or learning to be in the moment and see things "as they are"[44] and not be controlled by the "what if's" of the situation. DBT also seeks to establish the structure of relationships in healthier ways. Basically, DBT hopes to provide individuals with skills to manage stressful emotions and improve or reset troubled relationships.

DBT is an evidence-based therapy which can be helpful in recovering from codependency, along with many other things. The full DBT program includes an entire suite of approaches—individual sessions, group sessions, daily homework, and weekly phone call check in's under the supervision of a trained professional. However, in recent years some of the most helpful aspects of DBT have been made available in a variety of self-help books intended for individual use at home. One of the most helpful is *The Dialectical Behavioral Therapy Skills Workbook: Practical DBT Exercises.*

Attached: The New Science of Adult Attachment by Amir Levine

An entirely different approach to codependency comes in Amir Levine's book, *Attached: The New Science of Adult Attachment and How It Can Help You Find—and Keep—Love.* Amir's premise is this: Adults fall into 1 of 3 ways of relating to the world. They are either secure (about 50%

of the population), avoidant (about 25% of the population), or anxious (about 25% of the population.)

People who relate to others in a secure way feel good about their own ability to get close when needed and to have space when needed. They mostly focus on solving their own problems but are willing to help others with theirs under certain circumstances. They don't worry much about controlling others or trying to get their needs met through addictions or codependency.

People who have an avoidant style primarily operate out of fear of too much closeness. At first glance it might seem like these are unlikely candidates for becoming codependent, but it's not so. Every human needs connection, but when connection is also fraught with danger (of being hurt or rejected), humans need to find a way to be close without being *too* close. Some of them do this through becoming codependent and seeking to help and fix others instead of authentically getting close to them.

Others have an anxious style of relating. This type of anxiety is centered on being preoccupied with other people. The goal of the preoccupation is to make sure that the attachment to that person still exists—even if it has to be maintained through things like controlling them or fixing their problems.

When two individuals in a relation are both secure, things usually go pretty well. Both individuals know how to be close or have distance as needed and codependency probably won't develop outside of times of great crisis. Securely attached people often partner (in romance, friendship, business) with other securely attached people. This isn't always the case, but it is frequently so. This results in a high likelihood that the remaining 50% of the population, those who are either anxious or avoidant, will pair with each other.

When a person with an anxious attachment style partners up with someone who has an avoidant attachment style, things might not go so well. For example, when a stressor is put on the relationship, the avoidant person might do what avoidant people like to do—pull into themselves and hide for a bit so they can get their thoughts right. From the avoidant person's perspective, this is the logical thing to do. But their anxious partner might feel abandoned by this act. They feel upset that their partner has gone cold right when they were needed most. And in some circumstances the pair will develop a codependent style—the anxious one trying to pull the avoidant one out of their shell, or the avoidant one trying to convince the anxious one to change their ways and be more secure. This can also be termed a *pursue-withdraw* pattern. This can be a toxic combination that increases stress in the relationship.

The good news for individuals in this situation—and there are millions of them—is that individuals in partnerships or relationships can learn to see and accept both their own frailties and each other's. The anxious partner might be able to say to themselves something like, "When things get complicated my partner needs a few moments (hours? days?) to think. I can give them the gift of letting them have what they need." Or the avoidant partner can say to themselves, "My partner deals with stress in ways I don't understand, but I can't fix the issue for him/her. I will just try to be supportive along the way."

Levine's book, *Attached: The New Science of Adult Attachment,* helps flesh out this theory and how it can help people who struggle with codependency to conduct romance, friendship, or business in healthier ways.

Boundaries by Cloud and Townsend

One skill that both sides of a codependency must learn is how to navigate boundaries. Henry Cloud and John Townsend's book *Boundaries* is a great beginning text for this area. Most people have some idea what

re in a mental and emotional health context but little idea of
em in a helpful way. Often, it goes like this:

Person 1: I don't like when you yell at me. I want to
set a boundary so that it doesn't happen anymore.

Person 2: Okay.

3 days later...

Person 2 yells at Person 1.

Person 1: But I set a boundary for you not to yell at
me.

Person 2 shrugs.

This interaction is simplistic but all too often represents how
conversations about boundaries go. Somehow we think that boundaries
are intended to change another person's behavior. They are not.
Boundaries are for protecting ourselves.

Here is an example: You want to plant a vegetable garden, but there are bunnies and other creatures where you live. Just as soon as the tender shoots of vegetation break through the soil, a bunny will be there to have a nice snack. This is what bunnies do. If you want to keep the bunnies from eating your vegetables, you're going to need to put up a fence. You could spend a lot of effort trying to teach the bunnies not to eat your garden, but at the end of the day your garden will still be gone. If you want to protect your vegetables, you're going to have to put up a fence.

Boundaries work the same way in human relationships. You could spend a lot of effort teaching people around you how you want to be treated, but at the end of the day they get to choose their actions. A properly formatted boundary not only says, "I don't want you to yell at me," it also says, "and if you do, here is what will happen.... I won't feel safe sleeping next to you and will spend a few nights in the spare room." It is entirely up to the person who sets the boundary to carry out the actions needed in response to a boundary being broken.

Treatments for Trauma-based Codependency

Sometimes codependency develops in the context of trauma. Trauma changes people in lots of ways. And while everyone responds a bit differently to trauma, some common patterns emerge. One of those patterns is to take on some codependent behaviors. When one person is hurt through trauma, it is understandable to not want others to experience the same trauma. This desire to protect people from trauma can develop into a compulsive and anxiety-inducing codependency. For this reason, we are including a discussion about various ways trauma is treated.

Nick's story shared in the preface to this book is an example of how trauma can influence the development of codependency. For Nick, there was trauma associated by living life with a depressed spouse, along with the birth of children, loss of home, and economic instability mixed with the responsibilities of the Church—all these compounded events contributed significantly to the development of codependency. When there is pain, acts of charity and the accompanying feelings of goodness and love can serve to self-medicate the traumas of life. Whether major or minor traumas, each leaves its mark on the codependent mind. Like a moth to a flame, trauma-based codependency can often drive people to seek out others who experience trauma.

Trauma is just one way that codependency can enter the picture. There are plenty of others. Codependent trauma feels like the collateral damage of chaos. Therefore, if you control the chaos, you reduce the chance of further trauma. If you suspect that your codependency is rooted in or caused by a trauma you experienced, it might feel overwhelming to even begin to sort it out. It might be too big of a problem to tackle on your own. Thankfully in recent years a number of helpful therapies have emerged that can help—both for codependency and other situations.

EMDR

Eye Movement Desensitization and Reprocessing (EMDR) is a therapy developed in the 1990s by Francine Shapario. *Getting Past Your Past* is Shapario's text on the treatment. Although EMDR has been significantly expanded since its inception, her book is still the best beginning point for understanding what it's all about.

EMDR is an evidence-based treatment for Post Traumatic Stress Disorder (PTSD). During a typical session, clients work through the trauma or a dysfunction belief they developed because of the trauma. These traumas are processed in small sections until the distress caused by the event or thought is reduced. In short, the goal of EMDR is not to erase the past, but to disarm it.

EMDR is not a self-help treatment. You will need to work with a qualified mental health therapist who will help guide you through the process. It's not for everyone, but your therapist can help determine if it could be right for you. Not all therapists are trained in this technique, so if you are interested in it you will have to make sure the therapist you choose has the proper training.

(Side note: In the story used in the preface, EMDR is the treatment used to treat both Nick's wife for her depression and some of Nick's codependency. It is a powerful and relatively quick therapeutic approach. It may seem slightly unconventional when a patient first discovers and experiences it. However, this treatment has become a widely accepted approach to trauma-based issues.)

Brainspotting

One new treatment for trauma that is getting a lot of attention from therapists and potential clients alike is brainspotting. Invented in 2003 by Dr. David Grant, it is best described in his book, B*rainspotting: The Revolutionary New Therapy for Rapid and Effective Change.* Like EMDR, brainspotting attempts to access the places in the brain where memories of trauma are stored and help the individual process them more effectively. Brainspotting is different from EMDR in that it uses eye position to "spot" where issues are located in the brain. More research is needed, but initial studies seem to indicate that brainspotting is at least as effective as other evidence-based treatments.

Brainspotting is a therapist-led treatment. You can't read a book about it and do it on your own. As of the printing of this text, finding a therapist who is trained in this technique can be difficult. People living in major United States metropolitan areas are much more likely to find a therapist trained in this theory than people living in rural areas or outside of the U.S.

Cognitive Behavioral Therapy

Cognitive Behavioral Therapy (CBT) is the workhorse of the counseling world. Most licensed therapists use some form of CBT in at least some of their work. And while it is not as new and exciting as EMDR or Brainspotting, it remains beloved by therapists and clients alike because of its ability to create the climate needed for change. If you live in a part of the U.S. (or the world) where therapists trained in the new methods are generally not available, do not fear. Chances are great that a therapist near you practices CBT, and it can still be very helpful to you.

CBT is based on the idea that our thoughts, emotions, and actions are connected. When you feel inferior it is because you had a thought about being inferior. CBT goes to painstaking measures to name that thought, analyze it, figure out the ways in which it is defective, and replace it with something more helpful. If you can change your thoughts, you can change your emotions; changes to behavior will follow. This connects to trauma-based codependency because of the negative or toxic thoughts that can develop over the course of traumatic time periods or events. The impulses that arise as an answer to these traumas can be codependent in nature.

Seeking Therapy

Do I need a counselor? A therapist? A psychiatrist? A psychologist? What do all these titles mean anyway?

Making the decision to go to counseling can be hard enough. But often as soon as someone has made that decision they become overwhelmed by the many different titles and options. Adding further complexity, each state in the U.S. has its own requirements for each of these titles; outside the U.S. these titles may not be regulated at all. For some the decision about which type of professional to see is made easy: they consult the list of covered providers from their insurance and choose someone close to home who has openings that fit in their schedule.

———————

HOW DO YOU FEEL ABOUT SEEKING HELP WITH A
MEDICAL AND MENTAL HEALTH PROFESSIONAL?

———————

For others the choice is overwhelming. Here is a quick rundown of the differences between the various professionals you might consult for your mental health. But please understand that this is simplified in that each U.S. state has slightly different qualifications for each related title, and you should check with your state's professional licensing board if you want to know the specific qualifications of any particular professional.

Counselor vs Therapist: These two words mean essentially the same thing. If someone says they are a "mental health counselor" and another says they are a "mental health therapist," they are describing the same job. It's a bit similar to how some people call a sugary-carbonated drink "soda" and some call it "pop"—they are describing the same thing.

Licensed Counselor or Therapist: This is a person who has completed a master's degree in mental health counseling as well as other requirements, such as supervised experience and ongoing training. Licensed counselors can work independently (in their own private practice, for example) or can work out of an agency or setting. Counselors or therapists are generally not allowed prescription privileges, which means that if you decide to explore the use of medication to help with your mental health you will have to work with an additional professional to obtain a prescription. That professional might be your primary care doctor, an APRN, or psychiatrist (more on them below).

Licensed Counselor or Therapist Associate (sometimes also called Licensed Counselor Extern or Pre-licensed Counselor): This is a person who has completed a master's degree in mental health counseling and is still in the process of fulfilling post-graduation requirements. For example, many U.S. states require a counselor to obtain 3,000 hours of experience after graduation in order to obtain a full license. You might wonder why you would choose a counselor with less experience, and the answer often comes down to finances. Associate or pre-licensed counselors often charge a fraction of what fully licensed counselors charge. The risk that you take on by seeing someone with less experience is mitigated by the fact that these folks are also required to be under supervision of a fully licensed counselor.

Psychologist: A psychologist is a person who has more education than a counselor or therapist. We often call therapists and counselors master's level clinicians in contrast to psychologists, who are doctoral-level clinicians.

Psychologists receive more years in school and have a more rigorous training requirement. They are also different from counselors in that they can administer certain assessments such as IQ and more advanced psychological tests. Psychologists can work on their own (private practice) or out of an agency or hospital. Because they have earned a doctorate degree some of them use the title Dr., and some prefer to simply be called by their first name.

Psychiatrist: A psychiatrist is a full-fledged medical doctor who also has additional training in understanding mental and behavioral disorders. These are the "big guns," and they can help with anything from writing prescriptions to supervising patients who require hospitalization to treat their disorders. But what they don't usually do is therapy. If you want a person who will sit with you for an hour every week and help you sort through things, you are looking for a counselor, therapist, or psychologist. If you are looking for someone who can help you manage your mental health through physical means, such as prescriptions or other treatments that require a complex understanding of the physical body, you are looking for a psychiatrist. They are generally very expensive to see and can sometimes have a long waiting list for an appointment. As an alternative, you might consider seeing an APRN.

APRN for Mental Health: An Advanced Practice Registered Nurse or APRN is a registered nurse who also has a master's degree in the diagnosis and treatment of mental health issues. An APRN can write prescriptions and may work independently in a private practice, in a medical practice, or in a hospital setting. For many people who experience the more common types of mental health issues this level of experience is more than adequate.

So, which professional should you see? It depends on what your needs and goals are, and what your financial situation allows. In general, if you have never been to therapy before, you probably don't need to start with a psychiatrist. If you start with a counselor or therapist, they will have enough expertise to know if you need more advanced care.

How do you find a therapist? Your bishop might keep a list of professionals in your area, or he may invite you to visit the Church's Family Services. Please understand that Family Services is more of a short-term option, or is a referral service. Anyone needing long-term care will likely be referred to a full-time professional in your area. So, check with your bishop for a recommendation or consultation, especially if you are hoping to integrate your faith into your mental health. But you could also check with your primary care doctor, who probably has a similar list. Asking friends can be helpful, but sometimes people feel shy about seeing the same therapist as their friends. If your therapist is also seeing one of your family members or close associates, there are some notable ethical considerations to be considered.

However you proceed in this effort, we applaud your courage for seeking to improve yourself, or to at least become more familiar with these complex trials. This experience can be intense. In looking at the next steps we invite individuals to include their Church leaders, but with tender caution. No bishop or Relief Society president should be viewed as a mental health professional. Their calling and capacity are inspired and powerful, but it is unreasonable to think that a Church calling will convey 6+ years of college education and years of experience that mental health professions have earned. Consult with your leaders, but don't make your well-being their responsibility.

And a word about your bishop. Your bishop is likely not trained as a therapist. He may be an engineer or salesman by training. Don't let this dissuade you from speaking with him. Sometimes people make the mistake of thinking of their bishop as a second-rate therapist—someone who might be helpful and he might not, it's just the luck of the draw. But that's the wrong way to think about a bishop's role. A bishop has spiritual authority that a therapist does not have. Therapists have years of training in understanding human behavior, but they do not hold the keys that a bishop has. Even if you have a therapist, talking to your bishop may still be a necessary thing. He is there to help you discern, name, and repent of any sin that may be associated with your codependency. He can give you spiritual guidance on how to connect better with Heavenly Father. That's not your therapist's job: it is the job of your bishop, He is an advocate for you as you seek to live a healthier relational life.

Chapter 5: A Deeper Dive into Codependency

> "You find peace not by rearranging the circumstances of your life, but by realizing who you are at the deepest level."
>
> *Eckhart Tolle*

———◆———

Up to this point in the text you have learned what codependency is, and you can start to see how it manifests itself in spiritual and religious contexts. We have also given you some starting points on how to begin the process of healing, as well as some sources with which to address codependency. We would like to think that you are moving forward with a sense of hope, empowerment, and permission to make the changes towards a healthier place. These first four chapters should be sufficient to get you started on that path. However, if you feel that you want more, or if you feel there is a need to hone in on specific areas where codependency is most poignantly felt, we offer you the following resources.

This chapter is set up in alphabetical order and by areas where codependency might act as a trigger or is a contributing factor. The information is segmented and isolated by topic with no expectation of linear progression in the material. Consider it a reference guide in the many areas where codependency is manifest. *If you wish, you can skip this section and finish with the conclusion in Chapter 6.*

Addiction

Chemical, pornography, other process addictions, or even dietary addictions can be a manifestation of a deeper unmet emotional need. These can also arise as a result of previous and unmanaged codependency. Regardless of the cause of addiction, where there is addiction, there is like to be codependency nearby. The loved ones of an addict are likely to develop it, or the addict themselves became that way due in part to some aspect of codependency. The Church's 12-Step recovery program also has a companion program for individuals experiencing codependency. There is a free guide called *Spouse and Family Support Guide.* In some areas group meetings offer in-person support for people experiencing codependency as a result of a loved one's addiction.[45]

Spouse of a Porn Addict

Codependency is often an emotional response towards those for whom we care deeply. A common example of this form of codependency can be seen in the spouse of an individual dealing with pornography addiction. Pornography addiction is a process addiction, as opposed to chemical dependency like alcoholism. While it can be considered an addiction, it has become a prominent enough scenario that it is worth mentioning specifically.

Pornography addiction can be a sign of deeper emotional mismanagement or stress, but it is further complicated in that pornography distorts the reality of real-life relationships. When one spouse turns to pornography for self-medication from whatever emotional pain or trauma is present, the other spouse can take on some responsibility for that addiction. The victim-spouse may feel a need to change themselves or their actions with respect to their sexuality as a solution to the addicted-spouse's choices. This reaction is over-responsibility for the choices of the addict. In a rescue-type response to their spouse, the codependent will assume that their spouse's porn addiction was their fault in the first place and therefore they must save them from the addiction.

If this scenario involves a female spouse whose husband is addicted to pornography it is not uncommon for the wife to feel, "If I were more attractive or more attentive to his needs, his addiction wouldn't have taken place." Both spouses may find themselves feeling victimized, because the husband might agree or even communicate those ideas. The resulting bitterness can turn into anger towards one another for being perceived as insufficient. Eventually, codependency will most likely fail to repair the emotional trauma of the addiction and could be declared the *cause of death* on the autopsy table of their relationship.

The road toward healing here can be long and difficult, but not impossible. The spouse addicted to pornography can find healthier ways to manage their stress. Their spouse can make a strong internal boundary with themselves where they stop taking on responsibility for another person's sinful choices, no matter how personal that choice feels. Enlisting the help of your bishop, seeing a therapist, and reading helpful books can encourage you on your path.

Anxiety

Have you heard the saying, "Being angry is like drinking poison and expecting the other person to get sick"? When it comes to anxiety and codependency we might say, "Codependency is like regulating someone else's life and chaotic emotions and expecting your life to get calmer."

And it works! For a little while.

The codependent person finds themself in a cruel trap—their goals are being impeded by someone else's problems. This causes frustration, anger, anxiety, and even a sense of entitlement. Let's look at an example.

A Relief Society president has some anxiety about her new calling. She remembers when she was a girl her mother had been the Relief Society president for a time in addition to raising five kids, always looking tidy, offering hospitality in her home, and somehow managed to do it all without ever breaking a sweat. This newly called Relief Society president loves the gospel and her ward members and wants to make her Heavenly Parents proud. She also wants to live up to her mother's reputation and show herself as competent and worthy of her calling.

A few months into her calling she is not feeling that great about herself. It's hard to balance all her responsibilities and do the kind of job in her calling that she wants to do. And on most days she feels like at least someone in her life is getting short-changed, and all too often it's her kids. If she could just get her feet back under her, and start to have some success, she'd be feeling much better. And then, opportunity presents itself.

A sister in the ward calls her in crisis. This sister is a long-time member and a truly precious friend. Her husband died unexpectedly three years ago and since then everything has been a struggle, though many people in the ward help as much as they can. This sister struggles to put food on the table and often relies on using the local food bank located near her home. When she answers the phone the Relief Society president hears, "I'm so desperate to get some food in the house. Do you think you can help?"

Alarmed the Relief Society president immediately vows to help. But as she continues to listen on the phone, things get complicated. The sister in need says, "I just can't go to that food bank anymore. They don't have organic produce, only the regular pesticide kind. You don't want my kids getting cancer from pesticides, right? I need high-quality organic-certified vegetables for my kids. And I know I could go to the bishop's storehouse, but everything there is so bland and difficult to prepare. I just can't do it. Do you think you could arrange for people in the ward to bring me some organic produce? And maybe some organic meat too?"

The Relief Society president knows this request is going to be trouble. But as her anxiety rises she also thinks, "Well, I suppose I *could* send out an email and see if anyone has things to spare?" She silently reasons that this could be the situation where she can really prove herself. And when she does, all her feelings of anxiety about not being good enough will melt away. So she works hard and talks to ward members and even spends three hours driving to various members' homes to pick up the food they have to spare. When she arrives to drop off the groceries for the sister in need she expects to feel warm gratitude from this sister and finally know she is doing a good job in her calling. After unloading the groceries the sister in need says, "Well, I think this will last us about eight or nine days. When would you like to make the next delivery?" And the Relief Society president realizes the trap in which she's caught.

The problem is not that this kind woman who loves the gospel was trying to help a sister in need. The problem is that she was trying to make herself feel better by fixing someone else's problem. She had an unpleasant feeling inside of her (anxiety), and instead of doing her own emotional work to press through the feeling, she took on this sister's request hoping it would make her feel better. But instead it just created more problems for everyone.

Anxiety can come in other forms and is a legit medical and mental health concern. If anxiety is the motivating factor behind some of your Church service, it may be that there is a connection to codependency that should be explored with a therapist.

———————

WHEN YOU FEEL ANXIETY START TO RISE, WHAT'S YOUR GO-TO SOLUTION? DOES IT REQUIRE SOMEONE ELSE TO BE IN NEED? OR FOR YOU TO FIX SOMETHING ABOUT THEM?

HOW HARD IS IT FOR YOU TO SAY "NO" WHEN ASKED TO HELP?

WHAT DO YOU SEE AS THE VALUE OF PEOPLE LEARNING TO SOLVE THEIR OWN PROBLEMS? DO YOU SEE ANY TIMES YOU TAKE THAT VALUE AWAY FROM THEM BY SOLVING THEIR PROBLEMS FOR THEM?

———————

Cancel Culture

Cancel Culture is a term that has become such a part of modern society that the Cambridge English Dictionary has included this definition, "a way of behaving in a society or group, especially on social media, in which it is common to completely reject and stop supporting someone because they have said or done something that offends you."[46] While some argue that Cancel Culture has a place or function in society because it helps to remove offensive or problematic individuals from the mainstream, the mob mentality facilitated by social media tends to be a divisive battlefield of political and social ideologies that causes contention. Additionally, this mindset quiets individual freedom of expression and seems to be opposed to creating an environment where people can learn and grow, or experience the natural consequences of their choices. Individual choices become reasons to hate someone rather than simply disagreeing.

The intersection of Cancel Culture and codependency is where the actions/choices of others results in our decision (or compulsion) to control their actions. This includes instances where we have a strong impulse to fix the damage we feel they have caused. If someone on social media expresses an opinion that goes against our own position, do we see their opinion as harmful, damaging, or even evil, and feel some compulsion to make a campaign or join with others to not just disagree. Do we need to see that they are removed from employment, influence, or even membership in a group? If a celebrity states support for a political stance or candidate that differs from our own, do we counter their position with "cancel" hashtags to have them removed from a position influence? Do we boycott and maybe even seek to cancel our connections with like-minded people or organizations? Do we send out flurries of social media posts meant to convince our "audience" or circle of influence of the error of such thinking to save them from the harm such an opinion may have on society?

It is not uncommon for individuals on social media to respond and react more fully to political and celebrity controversies. Politicians and celebrities tend to be of the greatest influence and power in our modern society. As a result, some are even more scared to see that power used in ways that counter the narratives and principles that we wish to champion. We fear what may come from their influence going unchecked--so we feel compelled to act. While we can be suspicious of the motivations of others, to speculate and react to such suppositions may also be an act of codependency.

The Gospel of Jesus Christ is a gospel of forgiveness and repentance. Modern day revelation is quite clear on the principles we should follow by way of commandment: "My disciples, in days of old, sought occasion against one another and forgave not one another in their hearts; and for this evil they were afflicted and sorely chastened. Wherefore, I say unto you, that ye ought to forgive one another; for he that forgiveth not his brother his trespasses standeth condemned before the Lord; for there remaineth in him the greater sin. I, the Lord, will forgive whom I will forgive, but of you it is required to forgive all men. And ye ought to say in your hearts—let God judge between me and thee, and reward thee according to thy deeds."[47]

It has been said that we are in a time of "instant gratification." Search engines provide quick information, microwaves cook meals at rapid speeds, and entertainment is offered "on-demand." It would also seem that we have a desire for swift justice and perfection—now! This could be due to an intolerance of others, or of things we categorize as evil. For others it might be a need we have to feel morally secure or valued above others, thus the need to always vilify others so as to publicize our superiority.

In some instances this impulse to cancel or boycott those with whom we disagree is more about emotional management. By controlling the actions or consequences of others we experience less discomfort internally. We are unable to sit with the idea that someone who doesn't agree with our moral position could influence others to follow that same way of thinking. In order to not feel those fears, or to "save" others from that viewpoint, we cut the head off that monster before it can inflict others with their falsehoods.

The Atonement of Jesus Christ partially operates in linear time. Meaning, the Earth was created, and a mortality experienced, with the idea that we grow "line upon line, precept upon precept"[48] over a period of time. Additionally, "we see that death comes upon mankind, yea, the death which has been spoken of by Amulek, which is the temporal death; nevertheless there was a space granted unto man in which he might repent; therefore this life became a probationary state; a time to prepare to meet God; a time to prepare for that endless state which has been spoken of by us, which is after the resurrection of the dead."[49] Without linear time, when would we have the opportunity to choose and accept the Atonement of Jesus Christ, or to grow from mistakes?

The Plan of Salvation set forth by Heavenly Father, as opposed to the amendments put forward by Lucifer, gives space for people to grow and learn from error. To "cancel" people when they have done something in error, or even perceived error, places us in the judgement seat, and as the scriptures say leaves us with the greater sin. On some level, it seems to deny the power and purpose of the Atonement of Jesus Christ. Additionally, this tendency leads people to react codependently in order to reduce or eliminate future harm. But does it not cause more disharmony than it does good?

WHAT IS THE DIFFERENCE FOR YOU BETWEEN BOUNDARIES AND CANCEL CULTURE? ARE BOUNDARIES INTENDED TO PUNISH? IS CANCEL CULTURE INTENDED TO PUNISH? HAVE YOU EVER BEEN CANCELLED? HOW DO YOU WISH YOU HAD BEEN TREATED INSTEAD?

Church Callings

It is not uncommon to see employment and the demands of home and social life as drudgery. These responsibilities and seemingly unrelenting demands can leave members feeling as if they have been robbed of joy or the victims of a cruel world. Even Church callings can be performed as obligatory service in such a way that we give of our time reluctantly in an attempt to fend off guilt. In the end, what may have felt like guilt from the absence of action is replaced by resentment for offering a sort of compelled response. Some may end up feeling as if they are being acted upon rather than being able to act in a way that would bring them lasting joy.

Story and after story can be given where church callings have had a positive impact on both individual and collective development, and it is our opinion that a vast majority of callings are divinely if not charitably instituted for the improvement and benefit of the Church. Rare is the exception to this experience.

However, it is not the calling itself that can be the vehicle for codependency but how we approach the calling. With each calling comes a certain degree of responsibility. This responsibility is often spoken of as a set of people and tasks for which we are made responsible. The elders quorum president oversees the Stake's efforts for a particular ward in the stake. They lead and direct the efforts of the quorum, and they help train the priesthood holders in their respective sphere. Ward Relief Society presidents do the same for those in the ward's organized Relief Society membership. Their counselors help to counsel and sustain the president, and so on.

Along with these callings comes a sometimes heavy burden that weighs down or scares individuals. This emotional weight is accompanied by a sense of fear that the spirituality and righteous behavior of others somehow becomes their responsibility. If people don't come to church on Sunday, or if they don't do their ministering, we feel a sense that our eternal prospects are inseparably connected to their insufficiencies. In other words, we feel as if our moral success and the appraisal of our performance is dependent on the spirituality of those in our sphere of responsibility.

Church callings can be fertile ground for codependency because it creates opportunity for receiving positive rewards of service when other aspects of our life might be in pain or emotional strife. We minister to what can feel like an endless supply of people in need. It is not uncommon to find someone who is giving what might appear to be more than the average effort towards their calling, only to determine that their motivation for such diligence comes as a result of some loss or pain they are experiencing in their personal lives for which they are seeking emotional balm.

Ministering has been encouraged as a means of alleviating guilt rather than purpose for which it was divinely appointed. Other callings can also be promoted as the means of quieting the pains we might experience. In some ways these approaches may have merit, but for most it is not fostering a true spirit of chosen compassion.

When a child makes mistakes or goes through the steps of the learning process, it doesn't necessarily reflect negatively on a parent's ability to teach and guide. Similarly, a wayward individual in the gospel or in Church activity doesn't imply that a leader is bad or is failing. Sure there are instances where neglect is present, but doctrinally speaking, there is a limit to the responsibility of a calling that an individual has with regard to the actions and choices of others. However, many can view their sphere of responsibility as an over-responsibility for the choices of those for whom they minister.

Church service and Church callings should be accepted with a spirit of willingness and trust. Most callings require some degree of sacrifice. Self-sacrifice was not meant to be self-mutilation or self-destruction. Callings are about learning and growing, not controlling and mandating behaviors in others. Therefore, the quest to magnify a calling, or be successful in a calling, may lead some to control others into behaviors that grant the appearance of such success.

HOW DO YOU DECIDE WHEN TO SAY "NO" OR "YES"
TO A CALLING? IS IT EVER ACCEPTABLE TO TAKE ON A
CALLING, BUT PUT LIMITS ON WHAT YOU CAN AND
CAN'T DO? HOW FEARFUL ARE YOU OF OTHER
PEOPLE'S JUDGMENT THAT YOU MAY NOT BE SERVING
WELL? DO YOU EVER GET TEMPTED TO SERVE FOR
THE APPROVAL OF MAN AND NOT GOD?

Charity is divine and universal love. Charity is not a vehicle for guilt or punishment, nor is charity a drug used to numb the pains of mortality. Yet there are times where we have extended acts of service as the means of making ourselves feel better or as some sort of hope that by fixing someone else we are hoping to fix ourselves. Those who hijack and pollute this divine principle of charity as a war cry for compelling others to behave a certain way do so without the blessing of the Holy Spirit to confirm the truthfulness of their words. This fear tactic is employed when we are most afraid of the ways that people will use their agency.

President Uchtdorf counseled against this type of spiritual leverage: "Historically, fear has often been used as a means to get people to take action. Parents have used it with their children, employers with employees, and politicians with voters. Experts in marketing understand the power of fear and often employ it. This is why some advertisements seem to carry the implicit message that if we fail to buy their breakfast cereal or miss out on the newest video game or cell phone, we run the risk of living a miserable life, dying alone and unhappy. We smile at this and think we would never fall for such manipulation, but we sometimes do. Worse, we sometimes use similar methods to get others to do what we want. It is true that fear can have a powerful influence over our actions and behavior. But that influence tends to be temporary and shallow. Fear rarely has the power to change our hearts, and it will never transform us into people who love what is right and who want to obey Heavenly Father. People who are fearful may say and do the right things, but they do not feel the right things. They often feel helpless and resentful, even angry. Over time these feelings lead to mistrust, defiance, even rebellion. Unfortunately, this misguided approach to life and leadership is not limited to the secular world. It grieves me to hear of Church members who exercise unrighteous dominion—whether in their homes, in their Church callings, at work, or in their daily interactions with others."[50]

However, this idea of being over committed or compelled into acts of charity turn what should otherwise be a glorious and loving act into a compelled behavior that creates victims where there should be strengthening and kindness. If you are freely choosing to act in love, it is not charity. To paraphrase the scripture,[51] "Charity never forceth."

HAVE YOU EVER FELT BURDENED BY BEING ASK TO
DO SOMETHING OUT OF CHARITY THAT WAS TOO
MUCH? CAN YOU IMAGINE YOURSELF EVER SAYING
"NO" TO SOMEONE'S REQUEST FOR CHARITY? WHAT
ARE YOU DOING TO MAKE SURE YOUR TANK IS FULL
ON ITS OWN - SO THAT YOU WILL HAVE EXCESS
CHARITY TO OFFER?

Coworkers

The dynamics of work and office environments have a powerful social component. In some scenarios individuals spend more time with their coworkers than they do their family. Consequently, these situations can develop into relationships where deeply personal information is shared in an effort to seek compassion and empathy. Coworkers are a support system in ways that perhaps not even family may understand due to the complex balance that each must strive for between professional and personal. If unchecked, professional relationships can also become codependent.

No matter what your work environment—from being on a construction site to being in a 35th floor conference room—there is a certain joy that comes from working together with others to accomplish a task. The camaraderie of working side by side with coworkers is one of our joys in life. But it can also be one of the most challenging situations when roles are unclear, when a coworker is not taking care of their own responsibilities, or when one person tries to extend their authority beyond where it belongs. There are many ways this can play out, but let's just look at one: picking up the slack for a coworker who doesn't do their job well.

Dana is a paralegal and works downtown at a big law firm. She loves her job and feels like her contributions matter to the lives of the firm's clients. The firm employs 10 paralegals with varying degrees of experience—and motivation. The paralegals are assigned to cases based on their experience and availability. Dana enjoys a challenge and likes to be put on cases where she can stretch her skills and learn new things. So she was excited to be put on the firm's newest case. But her excitement dwindled when she found out that Robert was the other paralegal assigned to the case. Robert had been at the firm longer than her and certainly had some experience she didn't. In the past Dana noticed that every time she worked on a case with Robert he tried to push most of the work to her. Last time they worked together was on a case involving a man who was injured while walking past a construction site. The construction company had opened up a hole in the sidewalk and didn't clearly mark it as being an open trench. The man fell in and broke his back, causing him to lose months of work. He and his family were evicted from their home, and they suffered greatly. Dana was passionate about the case and helping this man and his family. So when Robert pushed his work to her, claiming to be too busy with other cases, she thought to herself, "If I don't do Robert's work too, we'll never win this case—and then what will happen to our client?" She felt stuck. She didn't have time to do Robert's work, but she didn't want to lose the case. At some point we are faced to make decisions based on the criteria, "is this my responsibility to fix?" In work environments we may not see compensation for being charitable, and we may not get a bonus for picking up another's slack. Nevertheless, individuals are faced with how their actions relate to their moral character as well as how their action (or inactions) may impact others. Adding the dynamic of commerce can impact our decisions in ways that may develop codependency.

HAVE YOU EVER HAD TO COVER FOR SOMEONE ON A GROUP PROJECT BECAUSE THEY WEREN'T PULLING THEIR OWN WEIGHT? HOW MUCH RESENTMENT DID YOU FEEL? WHAT KEPT YOU FROM ALLOWING THEM TO TAKE THE CONSEQUENCES OF NOT DOING THEIR OWN WORK? ARE YOU EVER IN A SITUATION WHERE OTHER PEOPLE'S WORK CAN NEVER MEASURE UP TO YOUR STANDARDS SO YOU DO IT FOR THEM? WHAT DO YOU THINK MADE YOU COMPELLED TO DO SO? WHAT WOULD HAPPEN IF YOU LET THOSE PERSONS FACE THE CONSEQUENCES OF THEIR OWN ACTIONS?

Dating

If modern dating isn't the world's best set-up for codependent relationships, we don't know what is. Dating is good. It's necessary and it's supposed to be fun. And, when done right, at the end of the process you find your eternal partner. But the whole endeavor is also filled with dangers for the codependent person.

In the early days and weeks of a dating relationship, each partner is eager to find points of connection. No one (we hope) enters a new dating relationship trying to find the ways they d*on't c*onnect with their date. But given enough time, differences on important issues will appear and a choice must be made: Do I say how I truly feel, knowing the person I am dating feels differently? If I do, I risk rejection. Or, do I tell the truth about how I really see things and find out if it is okay for us two to have differences?

Sometimes, tragically, the codependent person decides how to proceed based on an effort to manage their partner's emotions or responses. At first it feels like a clever trick that yields great reward: "If I don't say what I really think, I won't upset them, and they won't have reason to reject me." But at the core this kind of thinking leads to trying to manage your partner's emotional world for them in hopes that you can do it better than they can! The codependent person says to themself: "I can't trust what they will do if they get upset, so it is my job to make sure they never get upset." In the best-case scenario, the couple figures out this dynamic and though honest conversation is able to correct it. In the worst case scenario this couple wakes up one day after two years of marriage,

138

feels like they don't know each other, and don't have the freedom to be who they truly are.

A healthy dating relationship must be a careful mix of allowing room for what attracts the other while also making room to be honest about what you really think and feel, and trusting that the other person's emotional response to you will also be filled with honesty.

One additional area of consideration is the individual who dates someone whom they perceive to be "broken." Call this the "knight in shining armor" scenario, or the "I can fix him" mentality; but at its core, dating is not to be an act of salvation from some desperate and lonely wasteland. Entering a relationship or even continuing a romantic relationship under the thought that true love requires us to change or save the other person establishes expectations that can be toxic. The "knight" may always find ways to see their partner broken. After all, without a broken partner they may not see themselves as having value. What if that partner "gets better?" If the element that was so foundational to the relationship is "fixed," is there still a relationship?

In Latter-day Saint culture there is a fairly challenging dynamic where codependency can manifest itself, and that is when one of the people in the relationship is a member of the Church and the other is not. Because of the teachings relating to temple marriage, or the sealing ordinance with all its crowning blessings, and the fundamental necessity for both people to be members of the Church, this is a more notable issue than it may be to those of other Christian faiths.

Some may even enter a part-member dating relationship thinking "one day they will get baptized and we will live happily ever after throughout all eternity." In the back of their mind, or maybe even in the front of their mind, that non-member partner will be deficient in one very critical area that is not so easily "changed." Dating to "save" your partner in a religious or even social setting is an act of codependency that establishes a sandy foundation for that relationship.

DO YOU EVER TAKE ON THE KNIGHT IN SHINING ARMOR ROLE AND LOOK FOR DATING PARTNERS WHO NEED YOU TO SAVE THEM? DO YOU FEEL THAT YOUR DATING PARTNER'S CHANCE AT ETERNAL HAPPINESS RESTS WITH YOU - MAKING MARRIAGE A FORGONE CONCLUSION INSTEAD OF ONE CHOSEN? DO YOU TRY TO HIDE YOUR REAL FEELINGS FROM YOUR DATING PARTNER IN ORDER TO "NOT ROCK THE BOAT" OR NOT SCARE THEM AWAY?

Depression

Major depressive disorder, clinical depression, or simply depression as it is commonly referred to, is a condition that is characterized by chronic sadness, loss of interest in daily activities, and even irrational feelings of guilt and anger to such a degree that one becomes shut off from the world or devoid of the desire to accomplish even routine activities. This sense of hopelessness and what appears as a preoccupation with avoidance can be caused by a number of factors. These factors range from genetic predisposition or other biological contributors to trauma-induced environments. An individual with depression may experience shorter periods lasting a couple months at a time (sometimes during winter months or in darker environments) to decades long bouts with unrelenting symptoms.

Elder Jeffrey R. Holland taught this regarding depression, "When I speak of [depression], I am not speaking of bad hair days, tax deadlines, or other discouraging moments we all have. Everyone is going to be anxious or downhearted on occasion. The Book of Mormon says Ammon and his brethren were depressed at a very difficult time, and so can the rest of us be. But today I am speaking of something more serious, of an affliction so severe that it significantly restricts a person's ability to function fully, a crater in the mind so deep that no one can responsibly suggest it would surely go away if those victims would just square their shoulders and think more positively—though I am a vigorous advocate of square shoulders and positive thinking!"

"No, this dark night of the mind and spirit is more than mere discouragement. I have seen it come to an absolutely angelic man when his beloved spouse of 50 years passed away. I have seen it in new mothers with what is euphemistically labeled 'after-baby blues.' I have seen it strike anxious students, military veterans, and grandmothers worried about the well-being of their grown children.

"And I have seen it in young fathers trying to provide for their families. In that regard I once terrifyingly saw it in myself. At one point in our married life when financial fears collided with staggering fatigue, I took a psychic blow that was as unanticipated as it was real. With the grace of God and the love of my family, I kept functioning and kept working, but even after all these years I continue to feel a deep sympathy for others more chronically or more deeply afflicted with such gloom than I was. In any case we have all taken courage from those who, in the words of the Prophet Joseph, 'search[ed] ... and contemplate[d] the darkest abyss' and persevered through it—not the least of whom were Abraham Lincoln,

Winston Churchill, and Elder George Albert Smith, the latter being one of the most gentle and Christlike men of our dispensation, who battled recurring depression for some years before later becoming the universally beloved eighth prophet and President of The Church of Jesus Christ of Latter-day Saints."[52]

Depression is rarely experienced in isolation. When a person has depression, those around them can develop codependency. Conversely those with depression can also develop codependent traits. Similar to the spouse of an alcoholic, when one spouse has depression, the other spouse tends to feel a compelling demand to "pick up the slack" of their depressed partner. Children of a depressed parent or parents can feel as if they have to grow up too fast, having their childhood years taken from them. This tends to be the result of a child's perceived need to manage the gap of unmet responsibilities that result during a parent's depression. Friends, co-workers, and those in wards and branches who associate with a depressed person might all become susceptible to developing codependency—because they care.

While care, concern, and charity are all noble characteristics, it is plausible that these efforts can be offered in less than ideal ways. Over extended periods of time, what was once offered as charity might begin to feel as obligatory service. Consider the scenario of a Latter-day Saint family with a depressed wife (dependent) and her husband (codependent) with a number of children. When the husband of a depressed wife feels as if he has to manage all household affairs, earn income for the family, care for children, and manage Church callings, all while being deeply concerned for the well-being of his partner, who is in the darkness of depression, it understandable that one would, especially over time, begin to feel resentment or bitterness about this scenario, yet feel devastatingly compelled to continue in service.

The husband can also feel as if he needs to apologize for his depressed wife, as if her behavior somehow reflects negatively on him. In this way the husband takes on not only the physical workload but also the emotional responsibility for the entire family. It is not uncommon for the husband to feel almost as if he is a slave in his own home. He may also feel like a bad father if he were to receive help. After all, it is his responsibility to provide. He may even feel as if his marriage covenants are being called into question. This codependent scenario is perhaps more common than we may realize.

For those who develop codependency while caring for those with depression, there is an additional and unique challenge. Depression can impact someone's personality to the point where an otherwise outgoing and strong willed person can appear to, at times, lifeless. Such a dramatic shift in character can lead the codependent person to feel trapped in a relationship with someone who is almost foreign. When this arises one's codependency takes on a more complex layer. The intellectual and emotional dissonance that a codependent can feel in this scenario can have a toxic impact on their emotional and spiritual well being as they can feel further victimized.

Depression can work the other way around too if two previously non-depressed people develop a codependent relationship with each other. A kind of situational depression may develop on top of the codependency. But there may be some underlying good news for this situation.

Our emotions have two jobs: they give us information, and they urge us toward action. Our job as adults is to decipher the message these emotions are giving us, and then decide if the action suggested in our feelings is wise or not. No emotion is bad or good in this sense, it is just giving you information. So, if you are in a relationship and discern that feelings of depression are rising in you because of the dynamics of that relationship, you have a very valuable piece of information. There are many aspects to depression, but it is at least partly about sadness. What information could the emotion of sadness be trying to give you? That something is not as it should be. It's like a dashboard indicator telling you that something deep in the engine is not right. One can use that piece of information to figure out what to do next.

Too often what happens is that people experience an emotion like sadness as being an absolute truth that simply must be lived with instead of being a very helpful tool showing you what is wrong. This is very different from saying that you can just snap out of your emotions. You can't. Your emotions are going to stick around until you hear the message they have to give you. You might need help deciphering that message or figuring out what to do next because of it, but viewing your emotions as helpful friends who have something to tell you can help you manage feelings of depression in a more helpful way.

In this example—feelings of depression coming on because of a codependent relationship—the sad or depressed feelings could be telling you something is wrong in the relationship, leading you to investigate ways to fix what is wrong.

HAVE YOU EVER BEEN CLOSE WITH A DEPRESSED PERSON? HOW MUCH PRESSURE DID YOU FEEL TO "SOLVE" THEIR DEPRESSION FOR THEM? DID YOU EVER FEEL LIKE YOU NEEDED TO "COVER" FOR YOUR DEPRESSED SPOUSE WITH YOUR FRIENDS AND FAMILY BECAUSE IT WAS TOO SHAMEFUL?

Distraction from Spiritual Things

One of the adversary's tactics to keep us at a distance from the things of God is to simply be a distraction. Addictive behaviors can damage spirituality in a number of ways. One way in which codependency can enact its damage is simply by being so consumed with fixing others that we completely neglect our own spirituality—or other aspects of our discipleship.

One example of codependency can be found in the New Testament. Jesus Christ came to a village where a woman named Martha invited him to come into her home, presumably to teach and fellowship with those inside. Martha's sister, Mary, sat at the feet of Jesus and listened to him preach. While Jesus taught, and Mary listened, the record states that "Martha was cumbered about much serving." Whether Martha was just trying to be a good host, to have a clean home, or to serve others who were there, she felt that she was somewhat of a servant-victim in that no one was helping her in these tasks. Martha felt responsible for the comfort of those present as if people would otherwise be disappointed with what Jesus was teaching if *she didn't* serve them. Martha even confronted Jesus with the intent to induce her sister, Mary, to come help with these tasks, saying, "Dost thou

[Jesus] not care that my sister hath left me to serve alone? Bid her therefore that she help me."[53]

Jesus answered in a way that perhaps Martha was not expecting, "Martha, Martha, thou art careful and troubled about many things: But one thing is needful: and Mary hath chosen that good part, which shall not be taken away from her." In a manner of speaking, Martha could be demonstrating a common example of a codependent disciple response. Serving others, taking care of guests, even doing other tasks considered culturally acceptable for a host to perform is not bad or inherently evil. After all, Christ's message is to serve one another. So how could Martha have been in error?

Martha wasn't being told that she was evil; she was being told that she was misguided in her efforts. Jesus did not condemn Martha for her choice but helped her to see that she was being overly responsible and misplaced the value of her chores over things of greater spiritual value. Additionally, Martha was feeling victimized by the actions, or rather inactions, of her sister. The tone of Martha's response would indicate some feeling that Mary's choices have become a burden to her and that she felt some need to pick up her slack. In this scenario, a codependent act became a distraction to things of a more eternal nature.

This is not to diagnose Martha as being codependent, especially not from three short verses of scripture. But this particular story demonstrates a form of a codependent act and its connected counsel. This simple story does show that there can be spiritual contexts for codependency that received some counsel from the Master himself. There are many ways in which the challenges of mortality can be categorized as less than ideal simply because they are a distraction from a holier way, not because that thing is inherently evil.

In what ways have you been a Martha? On Sundays are you so busy getting all the kids pointed in the right direction that it's impossible for you to gain some spiritual nourishment? When you listen to talks in Sacrament Meeting or General Conference how often are you thinking about how the talk could fix someone else - but not yourself?

Expectations

We all have hopes and dreams for what we wish our life to be. The perfect job, the perfect spouse, ideal discipleship, a well-stocked bank account and retirement portfolio. The prospects of the ideal life are alluring and can be motivating. But, what if you have worked at your job for years, always to be passed up for the promotion you think you deserve? What if you date hundreds of people, and the spouse you have built up in your mind never presents themselves to you? What if you live paycheck to paycheck, always striving for that winning lottery ticket? When unrealized hopes and dreams turn into "expectations," they can take on an air of intensity and desperation.

It may seem strange at first, but we can become codependent based on something that is not even reality; we can have an unhealthy relationship with unmet expectations. These ghosts of our future lives can haunt our present lives as the scary and looming specter of "what could be." In a desperate attempt to exorcise this persistent demon some will turn to controlling others to manage the anxiety of unrealized expectations.

In a relationship setting, one partner may have started off with the expectation that their partner will eliminate a certain behavior in the future. When that happens, then they will be happy. If after years of marriage that behavior doesn't change, some will turn to controlling behaviors to "fix" that unwanted characteristic of their partner in hopes of alleviating their own anxiety surrounding the unrealized expectation.

There are a number of ways in which unmet expectations can become a toxic influence. In a Church setting this could be viewing other members of the congregation who live below their potential, or who, perhaps unknowingly, share false doctrines in class, or who seem to continually make choices that draw on the Church structure rather than sustain it. When we expect the world around us to be perfect, or even just better than it currently is, we are "in other people's business" that we are not responsible to fix and that can induce stress in our own lives. In some very extreme ways, the burden of unmet expectations have caused some violent responses, including mass shooting, suicide, or various forms of abuse.

When unmet expectations shift from being a motivation for self-improvement and become an anxiety- and depression-producing filter on life, one may turn to codependent acts to manage the resulting anxiety. Whether these expectations are of ourselves, others, or the world at large, unmet expectations can become the area where their fixing powers will be unleashed.

DO YOU EVER FEEL FRUSTRATED WITH FAMILY OR
WARD MEMBERS WHO SEEM TO FREQUENTLY FAIL TO
MEET EXPECTATIONS? DO YOU FIND YOURSELF
JUDGING OTHERS FOR THEIR CHOICES TO HELP CALM
YOUR ANXIETY ABOUT THE SITUATION?

Faith Crisis

Our faith, or our covenant relationship with God and our trust in
Him, is established and fostered through the Church that he established
for that very purpose. When the imperfect humans in his Church act or
teach things that are in disharmony with something we feel internally, even
emotionally connected to, the resulting discord has been called a "faith
crisis." Some members of The Church of Jesus Christ of Latter-day Saints
have described themselves as experiencing a faith crisis either after
encountering information that challenges their beliefs or after being
presented with an emotional or physical trauma that diminishes trust in
their previously held construct of deity. It feels as if there is a perfect storm
of emotional, spiritual, and even intellectual waves crashing on the rocks of
our expectations—resulting in chaos.

These feelings are often painful because the dissonance of a faith
crisis seems to target comfort areas in a way that one's internal scaffolding
begins to falter. The individual experiencing a faith crisis can appear to
make their faith problems the responsibility of others. For those
ministering to someone experiencing a faith crisis, it is easy to feel a
double portion of passion to fix the pains they are feeling. A crisis of faith
can be an intense experience depending on the circumstances and

personality of the individual. Regardless of how people come to a faith crisis, it is very real for them.

Those who interact with their religion to some degree of cognitive or emotional dissonance can develop a codependent relationship with their religion, and perhaps even to God. "When the church changes this doctrine, then I will believe." Or with God, "When God blesses me with _____, then I will know God lives and wants me to be happy or faithful." To this Jeffrey McLellan offers this counsel, "We are not commanded to have faith in blessings but in the Giver of blessings. The first principle of the gospel is 'Faith in the Lord Jesus Christ,' not faith in a charmed life free from trouble."[54]

While God is able to bring order from chaos, a codependent person's reaction to this scenario is to not trust in things or people that they can't control or in things that don't offer immediate respite from the storm. Individuals in a codependent faith crisis are more likely to place a premium on alleviating the anxiety of the situation than they are on resolving the dissonance with God's guiding hand. Because faith is such a foundational part of our lives, it is understandable that a faith crisis is almost as scary and painful as the prospect of a spouse cheating on you. What can you trust if it is not the things that you have come to love and trust, and who now appear to have abused that trust?

When the doubt or crisis of faith is severe enough, or jolting enough that an individual leaves faith and family connections behind, those connections may develop a codependent response to fix or save that individual.

Faith crisis is by its nature a response to information or experience where someone feels victimized. As a result, they have an injury to their joy and their faith, as well as a battered trust of God and his chosen mouth pieces on Earth. Some who experience this type of faith crisis will even engage in blame shifting or in displacing responsibility for their faith on others. The faith of that individual is not a living faith that grows and evolves but is reactive and is acted upon.

The argument can be made that there is a relationship between faith crisis and the rise of social media use.[55] For the sake of this section, it is sufficient to say that many going through a faith crisis turn to social media to find others who feel similarly. This could be to perhaps justify their anxiety as something that is not just in their head but is indeed a real problem that others are also experiencing. Turning to others on social media is a lifeline some use to make their faith someone else's responsibility to fix. Some will shout to their online "friends" something

like: "I'M HAVING A FAITH CRISIS—EITHER VALIDATE ME, OR
FIX IT FOR ME."

A faith crisis is a multilayered and nuanced experience. This sense of
personal insecurity and anxiety is also alarming because that individual will
see their old life as dead or dying. The need to grieve for an old life is thus
combined with insecurity about who they are becoming. There is a sense
that they are forever changed in a way they didn't choose: "Life brought on
this faith crisis; I didn't ask for this." Because of this, it is best to not
respond codependently and seek to control their faith experiences as we
can't know the many layers that they are dealing with.

Individuals learn, faith grows and evolves, and life experiences are
meant to change us. It is not wrong or unhealthy to be affected by the
things we learn or live through. However, the degree to which these events
take control of everyday living can be an area of concern. A person can
experience a trial to their faith and not abandon their life and belief systems
or feel victimized by it. However, *crisis* becomes the designated term when
the scenario feels out of control, disorienting, or hopeless. When people
are victims, or where there is a crisis, codependents are there to fix it.
Codependents can be like the ambulance-chasing lawyers following
accident scenes, only they are seeking out life's traumas.

These trials of faith could surface due to the death or severe physical trial of a loved one. A person who is experiencing the loss of a loved one, especially if the timing of the death is unexpected, can cause individuals to question their previously held belief in God as someone who would not be the cause of such pain and perceived injustice. Another faith-eroding scenario could be financial trials or other temptations to abandon divine or noble priorities. Some may even consider the notion, "I pay my tithing, so why am I going through a financial trial?" In light of this scenario some might doubt the validity of God or the promises (even those not doctrinally based) they have heard in the past as proof against their reality.

Others feel a sense of guilt over sinful practices that seem to constantly inflict them. They may feel as if God is not helping them overcome their problems. They might even distrust the promise of repentance because they feel as if their sins are too grievous to be forgiven. In its own way, this is a form of blame shifting that is also unhealthy, unsupported by the teachings in the scriptures and by modern revelation. God does love us and is tutoring us through our trials, not necessarily eliminating them.

Responding to a faith crisis does not have to be as urgent as it may feel. The term *crisis* tends to invoke a sense of urgency that compels an immediate response. And the person experiencing it does feel a sense or urgency. While it is not out of line for one to offer a somewhat immediate response, the nature of that response is not meant to be a solution, but a balm.

If you are connected to individuals experiencing a faith crisis, it is not your responsibility to fix it. When you feel anxiety or a compulsion to jump in and save them from their crisis, be aware that such a compulsion may not be motivated by charity nor result in clarity of mind for determining best approaches. Do we need to minister to and be Christlike towards them? Sure, absolutely, no question. But what does that mean? To the extent that you *own* their future choices with a relationship to this faith crisis will determine to what extent you are responding codependently.

WHEN A FRIEND OR FAMILY MEMBER GOES THROUGH A FAITH CRISIS DO YOU FEEL THE PULL TO FIX IT FOR THEM? ARE YOU CONSTANTLY SENDING THEM TALKS, SCRIPTURES AND SONGS (THAT THEY DIDN'T ASK FOR) TO HELP THEM GET OVER THEIR CRISIS BECAUSE THE STRESS IS TOO MUCH FOR YOU? ARE YOU ABLE TO SHOW EMPATHY WITHOUT CHANGING YOUR OWN BELIEFS?

Family Circumstances

The ideal, perfectly behaved family has rarely existed during any age of this earth. "The ideal"–where there are no broken bones, no loss of jobs, no wayward teenagers, and where all members of the family love and share experiences in Christlike harmony–is without example in the annals of human history. The story of Earth's first family, Adam and Eve with their sons, Cain and Abel, fell short of "ideal" in that one son killed the other. This event ushered in the darkest of sins that this world could ever know.

No family, even the family Jesus Christ was born into, could be considered "ideal" by today's standards. Joseph, Jesus's Earthly father, died prior to Jesus's consecrated ministry. Jesus's birth has historically and traditionally been depicted as some of the humblest of circumstances. We even have some evidence that Jesus's parents didn't necessarily feel like perfect parents. They did walk halfway home from Jerusalem before they realized they had forgotten him at the temple after all. There were likely times of missteps or challenging learning experiences along the way.

Joseph Smith's family experienced many challenges of poverty and maltreatment and persecutions for decades. Several stories of the Latter-day Saint pioneers crossing the plains have been recorded that show trial and trauma to be commonplace. Many of the early Saints spent time in the valley of shadows. Righteousness or obedience, it would seem, does not grant a stay of trial or a bestowal of immediate perfection in circumstance. So it should not be surprising that all families experience some degree of challenge in their sojourn along the covenant path.

To act and not feel acted upon in our family circumstances almost seems as if such an ability to exercise patience and wisdom at home is the product of fiction. When families inevitably fall short of the ideal, it is not uncommon for children or parents to feel victimized by the choices of those to whom they are deeply connected. It is hard to not feel occasionally as if a family is a chain gang where the progress of the individual is slowed by the human anchors who halt progress for the entire group.

'The Family: A Proclamation to the World" teaches "that marriage between a man and a woman is ordained of God and that the family is central to the Creator's plan for the eternal destiny of His children. The divine plan of happiness enables family relationships to be perpetuated beyond the grave. Sacred ordinances and covenants available in holy temples make it possible for individuals to return to the presence of God and for families to be united eternally. Husband and wife have a solemn responsibility to love and care for each other and for their children. The family is ordained of God. Marriage between man and woman is essential to His eternal plan."[56]

In support of these principles, the same proclamation offers practices and counsel as to how to best achieve these ideals: "Parents have a sacred duty to rear their children in love and righteousness, to provide for their physical and spiritual needs, and to teach them to love and serve one another, observe the commandments of God, and be law-abiding citizens wherever they live. Happiness in family life is most likely to be achieved when founded upon the teachings of the Lord Jesus Christ. Successful marriages and families are established and maintained on principles of faith, prayer, repentance, forgiveness, respect, love, compassion, work, and wholesome recreational activities. By divine design, fathers are to preside over their families in love and righteousness and are responsible to provide the necessities of life and protection for their families. Mothers are primarily responsible for the nurture of their children. In these sacred responsibilities, fathers and mothers are obligated to help one another as equal partners."

The proclamation continues to outline some counsel and understanding for circumstances that fall short of the ideal: "Disability, death, or other circumstances may necessitate individual adaptation." That one short sentence leaves tremendous room for exploring and developing practices that meet the principles and doctrines already outlined.

"Other circumstances" that necessitate adaptation can be scenarios where family members may have chemical dependency, where there is a clinically depressed family member, or other conditions where the limitations of mortality seem to impede an individual from achieving the doctrinal ideal. In some of these scenarios, parents and children find themselves reacting to the circumstances of their family in a way that can be considered codependent. In fact, families might be the place where codependency is the most common because the relationships could be described as largely unavoidable. There are also legal and societal regulations that require family members to be responsible for the actions and choices of the family members.

DO YOU FEEL LIKE YOU COME FROM A LESS-THAN-PERFECT FAMILY? DO YOU FEEL LIKE THAT MAKES YOU AN ODD PERSON IN THE CHURCH? DO YOU EVER TRY TO CONTROL YOUR FAMILY MEMBERS IN A WAY TO PROTECT YOUR REPUTATION OR STANDING WITH OTHERS? DOES ANYONE IN YOUR FAMILY USE THE LINE, "BUT SHE'S FAMILY" IN ORDER TO GET YOU TO DO THINGS YOU OTHERWISE WOULDN'T WANT TO DO?

Friendship

Codependency gets played out in friendship too. By this point in your reading you have probably imagined many scenarios of how that can be true. A person prone to codependency may unknowingly seek out friendship from those who contribute to their addictive behaviors. For those who like to think of themselves as h*elpers,* this can be a problem. It's normal for friends to rely on each other. And in Church culture this has historically been highly valued. But it is worth thinking about w*hy y*ou want to serve your friends.

Consider this real-life example. I (Jennifer) live in an area of the U.S. where snow falls a couple of times a year, and it's a big deal when it happens. Schools close, employees work from home, and everyone is excited to go outdoors, try sledding, or look at the beauty the snow brings. Because it is a novel occurrence, many folks are not used to driving in the snow and attempt to stay off the roads as much as possible. Last winter, in the middle of the night and during such a snow event, we had a pipe burst at our house. Water was rushing into an interior wall. My husband and I are not particularly handy with household tasks, but we knew enough to know that the water had to be turned off. The problem was, we didn't know where the shut-off valve was located. While water was still gushing we looked in the logical places and didn't find the valve. I pulled out the documents and schematics we had filed away about the house, but in my panic I wasn't able to learn anything.

Meanwhile my husband was searching the internet for "how do you find the water shut-off valve." Nothing of help. In a moment of desperation, I remembered that many of my ward members lived in houses built by the same builder. Perhaps one of them would know how to turn the water off. But it was after midnight and I was skeptical anyone would be awake. I fired off a panicked-sounding email to our ward email list explaining our situation in a sentence or two. Within just a few moments my phone was ringing, "Is the water still going? Okay. My husband is on his way over. He'll be there in 2 minutes." Shortly after that emails poured in with ward members offering to bring by dry towels, drying fans, or whatever else was needed—even though it was the middle of the night, and even though we were having snow.

In this example we had a real crisis and needed real help. People jumped to our aid, and it was appropriate for them to do so, even if it was the middle of the night. We come from a faith tradition that knows how to help in a crisis. We also have many examples in our Church of long, sustained friendships between individuals and families, relationships that are not formed around crisis. We are simply brothers and sisters in the Lord, being in each other's lives like family. These are good and precious things. It would be wrong to read codependency into those healthy friendships. In that sense, we don't see codependency hiding under every rock, nor do we find in every relationship something that needs to be pathologized. Friendship is good. Helping is good.

Codependent relationships are driven by unmet needs. Codependency is not one person being in need in the middle of the night and another coming to help. Codependency is not friendships sustained over the course of life where each individual supports and sustains each other. Codependent friendships are driven by the need of one (the codependent) to fix the other so that the codependent feels better about themself, their situation, their life. A desire to help another is good, but it gets twisted and misshapen if it is driven by a need to feel better about one's self.

The natural question you may be asking yourself is: How do I know if my friendship is codependent or not? And while that is a legitimate question, it's one that's hard to answer. If you suspect that a certain friendship might be codependent a better question might be: Can I identify ways in which parts of this friendship are codependent? Rarely is a friendship just one thing, and the relationship you are wondering about might be made up of lots of healthy parts alongside some less than healthy parts. Here are some other questions that might help you discern what elements of codependency exist in your friendship:

Do I hold imaginary conversations in my mind with this person where I try to convince them that I can help them with a situation or relationship? Or where I offer the perfect solution for them, if only they would listen to me?

How do I react when this person doesn't take my advice and makes choices I consider foolish?

Does my anxiety increase when they don't take my advice?

Am I so invested in helping this person that it is hard for me to take care of other things in my life that really need my attention?

These questions can be difficult to explore. These questions are not usually answered with a simple "yes" or "no." They are meant to help you explore the nature of your friendships. This work might be benefited with the help of a trusted friend, bishop, or counselor to work through them. The good news is that friendships can heal. Codependency can be reversed, and you can learn healthier ways of relating.

Gender Differences

Mental health issues can manifest in different ways based on gender. While these differences are rarely gender exclusive, one must be sensitive to these differences to diagnose the situation properly. We don't always diagnose men with codependency: we say they are angry. However, it may be helpful to explore a possible connection between their anger and codependency. Women may "wear it more on the sleeves," while men may display behaviors that appear symptomatic of something else. And there are some good reasons why this is true. Gaining some insight into how gender influences the expression of codependency can keep you from developing a stereotype of what codependency looks like.

A full exploration of how gender impacts codependency requires additional research and may be best administered under the care of trained professionals. However, we encourage the process of discovery of any undesirable or negative behavior as it is analyzed through the lens of codependency. Stereotypes, including those based on gender, may be the result of codependency. This is not to say that all such behaviors are codependent, but it is worth considering such things as codependency is treatable.

Law of Consecration (Doctrine and Covenants 119)

Through the influence of folklore and other cultural influences, some have developed an incomplete or inaccurate perception of the law of consecration as well as when it became "a law." The law of consecration is given by way of covenant. Those who enter into that covenant make a commitment that doesn't imply a specific action but rather a willingness to live the principles of the law in whatever form those principles may present. The definition of consecrate or the law of consecration is "to dedicate, to make holy, or to become righteous. The law of consecration is a divine principle whereby men and women voluntarily dedicate their time, talents, and material wealth to the establishment and building up of God's kingdom."[57]

Nowhere in this definition is there mention of the ownership of property. Two people could have the exact same possessions or amount of property, and one could be living the law of consecration and the other could not. The principle is based on one's commitment to make something holy or to use their time, talents, and anything the Lord has given them responsibility over for his divine purposes. There have been instances in Church history where transfer of title or property rights to the Church were given freely in accordance with this law, but it is not a requirement for all, nor is the transfer of property ownership the only form of consecration.

One of the inaccuracies that some teach regarding the law of consecration is that an individual or family covenants to give literally everything that they own and possess to the Church or to the service of others. This sort of communal ownership, especially when done as some sort of tax to enter a different degree of citizenship in the kingdom of God, is not accurate. In fact, the language of doctrine and Covenants section 119 seems to suggest that maintenance of private property is a critical component of consecration as it dovetails with the principle of moral agency and stewardship. The scripture reads, "Verily, thus saith the Lord, I require all their surplus property to be put into the hands of the bishop of my church in Zion." Stating that a "surplus" is to be given to the Church implies that there is a portion that is not required under this law. This distinction also gives each individual the divine opportunity to reason with God as to what is considered a necessary amount of property and what is considered a surplus.

How does the law of consecration relate to codependency? Outside of property, something which is measurable as far as amount and value, the law of consecration also talks about dedicating our time and talents. Because these things are harder to quantify, it can also be hard to determine if you have given too much of yourself until you have passed that point. If your perception of the law of consecration is that you are to give everything you have and keep nothing for yourself, you may feel compelled to, as the scriptures state, "run faster than you have strength."[58] Because this is a covenant, there is a certain degree of moral accountability that can cause one to over-give in a compulsive manner, especially if one is experiencing a trauma or trial where they see such sacrifice as a prerequisite for additional blessings which they are desperate to realize.

Joseph Smith taught this to the early Saints, "I will tell you that every man must be his own Judge how much he should receive and how much he should suffer to remain in the hands of the Bishop. I speak of those who consecrate more than they need for the support of themselves and their families the matter of consecration must be done by the mutual consent of both parties for, to give the Bishop power to say how much every man shall have and he be obliged to comply with the Bishops' Judgment is giving to the Bishop more power than a King has and upon the other hand to let every man say how much he needs and the Bishop obliged to comply with his Judgment is to throw Zion into confusion and make a slave of the Bishop the fact is there must be a balance or equilibrium of power between the Bishop and the people and thus harmony and good will may be preserved among you."[59]

The law of consecration has been required of the disciples of Jesus Christ since Adam and Eve. This again is a true principle, one that pertains to our salvation, and has continued to be taught by the leaders of the Church. At the heart of the law of consecration are the "two great commandments": to love God, and to love our neighbor. Accordingly, we are taught that in order to love God we must possess a trilaterally equal love for God, our neighbor, and ourselves. These are not mutually exclusive priorities, but they do, at times, seem to compete with one another. Consequently, the law of consecration can, at times, feel like we are being asked to throw off that balance, when it is that balance that defines true consecration—to make ourselves and others around us more holy.

HOW WOULD YOU DEFINE THE LAW OF
CONSECRATION? IS THAT DEFINITION SUSTAINABLE
FOR YOU? DO YOU APPLY IT TOO HARSHLY TO
YOURSELF? OR TO OTHERS? DO YOU EVER FIND
YOURSELF TRYING TO GIVE OUT AN EMPTY BUCKET?

Missionary Work

Full-time missionary service is an area where certain approaches can develop an environment of codependency. Like in other areas of this text, we hope to discuss this subject matter not as a criticism of official teachings or practices. We hope to wipe the dirt and grime off the lens we may use to see these topics, and thus perceive with increased clarity.

Missionary work is a key part of discipleship. The effort to bring the gospel message and its saving ordinances to the world is empowering and is the method of saving the world from its fallen condition. It is a most noble work in which to be engaged.

How an individual goes about doing missionary work can be effective and enlightening, and it can also be a stressful, guilt-ridden set of compulsive behaviors designed towards being found spotless at the last day. Why one decides to do missionary work could very well be the reason some are so reluctant to take part in the effort.

The natural inclination in this spot is to talk directly to those serving full-time proselytizing missions. After all, this is a calling where an individual must learn to balance an intense version of living the law of consecration (please see that section earlier in this chapter), as well as do things like goal setting where the goals are largely measuring the agency of others. But these principles can apply to all who call themselves disciples who engage in missionary work.

If you set a goal to teach two or twenty lessons, your goal is largely in the hands of the people whom you invite to accept your invitations. If you miss those goals, it is not uncommon for guilt to take over. Guilt is a powerful motivator, but it is not a divine one in most cases, especially when that guilt is born of consequences not of our own choosing. Outside of hours spent in proselytizing and in service efforts, perhaps even in fulfilling study time requirements, there are few ways that a missionary can measure their efforts without being at risk for misplacing their value or their influence on something external, and, as a result, develop a sense of codependency through their service.

One can expend their "heart, might, mind, and strength" in the service of others and see no baptisms, no re-activations, not even one sympathetic ear, and still be a successful missionary. While some have presented that idea, it is not always commonly applied in the field. Many examples can be given in the scriptures of people who were great missionaries, but who had few, if any, converts to show for their efforts. Abinadi in the Book of Mormon is one such example. He literally sacrificed his life in teaching the gospel, a very literal example of consecration. Even if Alma had not been converted by the words of Abinadi, Abinadi did as he was commanded, and in that he fulfilled the measure of his creation.

There is enough anecdotal evidence to support the idea that some have sought to motivate individuals to do missionary efforts by emphasizing each individual's responsibility for those to whom we *can* teach the gospel. This responsibility has been described as an absolute: "If you don't share the gospel with them, you are responsible for their salvation—so open your mouth!" This scripture is one used to push that narrative: "And now, my beloved son, notwithstanding their hardness, let us labor diligently; for if we should cease to labor, we should be brought under condemnation; for we have a labor to perform whilst in this tabernacle of clay, that we may conquer the enemy of all righteousness, and rest our souls in the kingdom of God."[60]

Jacob in the Book of Mormon also taught, "And we did magnify our office unto the Lord, taking upon us the responsibility, answering the sins of the people upon our own heads if we did not teach them the word of God with all diligence; wherefore, by laboring with our might their blood might not come upon our garments; otherwise their blood would come upon our garments, and we would not be found spotless at the last day."[61] In light of these two verses, it feels hard to come to any other conclusion—we are responsible for the salvation of others. So, is this one area where doctrine and codependency don't line up?

It is not in the authority of the authors of this text to expound and clarify the Church's position on these matters. This is a matter of personal revelation, and we encourage individuals to be prayerful in coming to some understanding of how these verses apply to each individual situation. Where there is a responsibility, there is accountability. To what extent that accountability extends to the actions of the people whom we teach is another matter. We suggest that there is a difference between our responsibility to teach and the responsibility to accept that message.

Please consider this encouragement regarding how one reads the scriptures: the text can be d*escriptive,* and it can be p*rescriptive.* D*escriptive* here means that what is written is simply describing what the people were doing or how they felt. P*rescriptive* means that the author, or perhaps the Spirit, is giving words of counsel to encourage the hearer or reader to certain actions or beliefs. When a scripture can be considered one or the other may shift from moment to moment depending on the workings of the Spirit or the context of the verse. In these scriptures from Jacob or Moroni, they felt an acute and distinct responsibility for the people for whom they had influence. They were not necessarily advocating that the reader has that same degree of responsibility for every person whom they encounter.

Where there is opportunity and ability to serve, these scriptures are congruent with the principles of discipleship that state, "Now let every man learn his duty, and to act in the office in which he is appointed, in all diligence. He that is slothful shall not be counted worthy to stand, and he that learns not his duty and shows himself not approved shall not be counted worthy to stand."[62]

But this must also be balanced with the scriptures that call for a wise effort and reasonable understanding. No individual on this planet gets only one chance to hear and accept the gospel message. We must also be careful to not overreach in matters of accountability. Because some see conversion and baptism as the only legit sign that we were sufficient in our effort to teach others, we can often assert a responsibility in missionary work that implies that without a baptism we have not been sufficient, and therefore a heavy weight of sin is placed upon our heads. We simply invite people to consider the impact such teachings might have on the people for whom the counsel is directed and apply the doctrine in the correct spirit.

AS A MEMBER-MISSIONARY, DO YOU EVER FIND YOURSELF CULTIVATING RELATIONSHIPS WITH COWORKERS OR NEIGHBORS SIMPLY BECAUSE YOU WANT THEM TO "SAVE THEM?" WHEN YOU'RE TALKING WITH SOMEONE ABOUT THE GOSPEL ARE YOU ABLE TO RECOGNIZE THAT THE SPIRIT DOES THE WORK - AND NOT TRY TO LIVE BY SOME PREDETERMINED AGENDA OR OUTCOME? DO YOU STRUGGLE WITH FEELINGS OF GUILT THAT YOU'RE NOT "MAGNIFYING" YOUR CALLING OR MISSIONARY WORK ENOUGH?

Ministering

Some of the ways codependency might present itself can be seen in our ministering (formerly home and visiting teaching). Ministering closely resembles the issues that we discuss in the section on missionary work.

The same core questions regarding motivations can apply. Why should one minister to others? A common answer is "because God asked us to." The best answer is "because I love them and want to support them on their own path back to our heavenly home." However, a codependent might answer, "Because they are not living up to their potential, and they need my help to get out of the path of sin and unhappiness."

Additionally, a codependent might minister to others because their own home lives are such a mess that, maybe, if they go out and try to fix someone else's life, by extension their lives won't seem out of control. If this sort of motivation becomes the "norm" or is the persistent motivation for why one does acts of discipleship, it could lead to associating guilt with holiness.

In Church responsibilities, individuals can sometimes feel crushed under the weight of all the demands on their attention. This becomes a particularly painful confluence of emotions when ministering is seen as an assignment to "fix" those for whom we have a relationship of care. What if they don't become "all better" in the time frame we think they should? That sense of urgency for people to "get better" can be a form of over-responsibility and likely comes from one's own need to see change so as to relieve their personal pain of suffering for and in behalf of others. While a disciple of Christ will want to help people improve the quality of life and to alleviate suffering, Christ never placed the responsibility for the "results" of our ministering on anyone else.

Using charitable efforts as a weapon to combat internal pain is a dangerous path that can lead individuals to see the pain of others as an opportunity for a spiritual high. This can lead an individual to create drama where there isn't any simply to feel a temporary sense of purpose and self-fulfillment. Ministering is focused on the individuals for whom we minister. When ministering turns inward, we should be aware of codependent feelings that may arise.

Questions to consider: How do you decide what level of help you will give those to whom you minister? When you are ministering to someone how much do you have your hopes set on a certain outcome for them? When you minister to someone who is, "not living up to their potential" how uncomfortable are you? How much do you try to fix that for them?

Music and Lyrics

Music and movies for decades have been forwarding a definition of love that has informed the way we aspire to be. Some songs illustrate dramatic and over the top, almost desperate emotional language with such regularity that its not hard to see this romanticized experience of saving broken people or struggling relationships as "true love." Here are few examples:

"I watched you sleepin' quietly in my bed
You don't know this now but
There's somethings that need to be said
And it's all that I can hear
It's more than I can bear

What if I fall and hurt myself
Would you know how to fix me?
What if I went and lost myself
Would you know where to find me?
If I forgot who I am
Would you please remind me?
Oh, cause without you things go hazy"[63]

This is a beautiful song, and the spirit of the message could be interpreted as people expressing passion and connection to each other. But it also sends a message of dependency, or that their idealized romance requires a degree of broken-ness that is "fixed" by the other person. the melody's and performance are real, beautiful, and feels genuine--a sweet sentiment that packages less than healthy lyrics.

Here is another popular song with an all too common sentiment:

"Baby love, my baby love
I need you, oh how I need you!
But all you do is treat me bad
Break my heart and leave me sad
Tell me, what did I do wrong?
To make you stay away so long

'Cause baby love, my baby love
Been missing ya, miss kissing ya
Instead of breaking up
Let's do some kissing and making up
Don't throw our love away
In my arms why don't you stay?
Need ya, need ya, baby love, baby love

Baby love, my baby love
Why must we separate, my love?
All of my whole life through
I never loved no one but you
Why you do me like you do?
I get this need

Need to hold you, once again, my love
Feel your warm embrace, my love
Don't throw our love away
Please don't do me this way

Not happy like I used to be
Loneliness has got the best of me

My love, my baby love
I need you, oh how I need you!
Why you do me like you do?
After I've been true to you
So deep in love with you

Baby, baby, 'til it's hurtin' me
'Til it's hurtin' me, baby love
Don't throw our love away
Don't throw our love away"[64]

This song is considered a classic, and one that influenced many other "love" songs. In many ways this is a great tune, but the text itself speaks to a common view of "love." The idea that a person is miserable in their relationship but can't seem to function independently of the other person who is simultaneously making them miserable and happy at the same time. This certainly doesn't represent the ideal, few love songs do. Song lyrics tend to be glamorizing negative things, or over dramatizing and inflating the drama rather than displaying ideals.

Perhaps the most codependent love song lyrics can go to the song,
"When Something Is Wrong with My Baby":

When something is wrong with my baby
Something is wrong with me
And if I know that she's worried
I know I'd feel the same misery

We've been through so much together
We stand as one, and that's what makes it better
When something is wrong with my baby, people
Something is wrong with me--

Just what she means to me,
now oh, you just can't understand
People can say that my woman, she's no good
But she's my woman and I know I'm her only
man.

And if she's got a problem
Oh, I gotta, I gotta help her solve them
When something is wrong with my baby
Something is wrong with me

I gotta tell it to ya just one more time
When something is wrong with my baby,

something is wrong with my baby
When something is wrong with my baby,
something is wrong with me. "[65]

This song was so popular that it was recorded by a number of artists across a couple of decades. This song idealizes a level of commitment that presupposes complete dependency on the happiness of the other partner. When a romantic partner is almost subservient to the problems that another person experiences, this is codependency.

There are scores of songs that perpetuate this idea that love requires some kind of lose-win scenario, or where true love is defined by some level of dependency or lost self or it isn't real.[66]

Parenting and Transitioning Children to Adulthood

Some parents are constantly scared about the decisions of their children. Others seem to accept some degree of failure and missteps along their path of growing up. But for those who deeply wish to protect their children from potentially harmful life choices (some call this helicopter parenting), there will come a time where the child will need to leave the home and start a life of their own. Rather than control children to mirror our actions or push them to be puppets acting out the fantasy life we have envisioned for them, God expects us to tutor them and guide them.

Parenting is a difficult area to navigate when it comes to codependency because our children are, in many ways, dependent on their parents. Therefore, being responsible for them is natural and expected. But children also need space to grow, which includes a fair amount of making mistakes. So, learning how to balance healthy boundaries with our desire to protect our children from the experience of pain or extreme struggle can be challenging.

Children may not be able to accumulate financial means nor are they likely to manage those resources well if acquired. Additionally, their emotional and physical needs require the guiding hand of an experienced adult to care for them without irrational indulgence or cold indifference. This level of dependence is compounded by the idea that responsibility for the spiritual and temporal welfare of these children is a matter of our standing with God. Feeling this enormous weight can be difficult to manage without developing some sense of codependence.

Additionally, there are scriptures that emphasize this great moral accountability for how children are raised with some heavy warnings attached. The Doctrine and Covenants states: "And again, inasmuch as parents have children in Zion, or in any of her stakes which are organized, that teach them not to understand the doctrine of repentance, faith in Christ the Son of the living God, and of baptism and the gift of the Holy Ghost by the laying on of the hands, when eight years old, the sin be upon the heads of the parents."[67] This added measure of doctrinal weight on our parenting may compel us to control our children's behavior as some method of removing the chance of our own failures..

In response to this heavy load, some parent their children so as to control or compel them into certain behaviors. At times, this can be done to alleviate the emotional pain that results from their children's decisions to be disobedient. In other words, sometimes people parent not because it is good for the child, but because it will help the parent feel less like they messed up or that they may be a bad parent.

Sometimes parents assume that their children are, and always will be, broken, so they expect failure. Codependent parents often feel a need to keep seeing their children as broken and perpetually needing their parents to fix their problems. In this we must remember that we are commanded to forgive all, which includes our children.[68] For some, this constant disappointment in their children can take on a level of emotional abuse, especially when the parents engage in commentary on the child's life that implies that they will always mess things up because they always

185

have. If you say this to your child, you are in danger of being emotionally abusive towards them. The damage that results from such abuse will likely increase unwanted behaviors.

Author and historian LeGrand L. Baker illustrated how a proper parenting pattern was applied in Moroni's angelic tutoring of the Prophet Joseph Smith prior to the formal establishment of the Church in 1830. History shows that from the time Joseph experienced what has now been called "The First Vision" at age fourteen in 1820 and the time he established the Church ten years later, he was learning to find this balance between being a prophet of God and being himself. The angel Moroni visited Joseph on several occasions. Joseph grew from Moroni's instruction. He learned a great deal about himself, and about what it means to be a prophet. LeGrand Baker writes, "God expects one to make intelligent, well informed decisions. If those decisions are incorrect, then the Holy Ghost will sound a warning, but prophets do not just sit around and do nothing until they get instructions. Moroni taught Joseph to be a prophet, not a puppet. A prophet and a puppet are not the same thing. When our sense of right and wrong is correct and embedded into our personality, the consequence is happiness and security in our relationship with God. A major purpose of the Holy Ghost is to facilitate an understanding of one's Self by one's Self, so that within the full scope of one's own strengths, one can make and act on correct decisions—knowing always that the Holy Ghost will sound a warning if the decisions are not correct."[69]

When parents are overbearing and seek to control the behaviors of their children or to shelter them from the pains of mortality, they are raising a puppet, not a person. These behaviors will result in moral atrophy as individual children will not know good from evil through their own experience. These children will simply be tossed by the whims of their parents or by the currents of social culture.

Children transitioning to adulthood represent the last stages of parenting as well as the slow introduction to being more fully on their own. This can be scary for both parents and children, but it is also an important time. It is of no coincidence that our Heavenly Father wants his children to be close to him and be engaged in missionary service at this stage of their personal development. Micromanaging this time is a difficult proposition, but it does require great care to allow this time to be most effective. Children will make mistakes throughout their lives. But the time when transitioning children into adulthood is a time where children most need the freedom to act, while still having some degree of a safety net for any significant falls. What they don't need is coercion and heavy-handed dictatorship-style parenting.

Just as Joseph Smith had missteps in his life even under the direction of the angel Moroni, young adults need help navigating the difficult relationship that is this marriage of their eternal and individual self with their divine nature and potential. This requires self-discovery and positive reinforcement. Efforts to control or fix their life decisions may short-circuit the very thing you wish to happen.

Joseph Smith was asked how he was able to govern many people and keep order among the Saints, to which he responded, "I teach them correct principles, and they govern themselves."[70] It is likely that this is how Joseph learned under divine tutelage and knew firsthand how powerful this method can be. This pattern of teaching principles, then giving individuals the space with which to come to a deeply personal testimony of their truthfulness, is applicable to parenting and governance in the home.

However, this principle is not easily put into practice. Often either parents don't teach the principles sufficiently, in both word and in deed, so that the children are left to govern themselves with sufficient instruction, or they are not given the chance to govern themselves due to a controlling degree of oversight and a parental need to coerce their decisions through various forms of punishment. In the case of the latter, we can see how codependency can govern the parent in ways counter to prophetic principle.

What Joseph Smith taught was not meant to demoralize our existence or to eliminate sin. Rather, given the context, he was teaching how society may avoid codependency and more fully realize the unifying and empowering principles of interdependence. When parents over-parent, over-correct, and take on more roles and responsibilities than they are able, codependency is likely to result. When children are absolved of the consequences of their actions because parents fear how the parents are liked or perceived by their children, this could also be developing a codependent relationship between children and their parents.

Some parents choose to misplace their affection by buying many things for their children as a token of their good parenting or a symbol of their grand ability to provide. In so doing, these parents deny their children the principles taught in the law of the harvest, an eternal and unchanging law. The same can be said for parents who provide emotional triage and shelter their adult children who are otherwise capable of providing for themselves. Parents are no more responsible for living the life of their children than God is for living our lives. Because codependence is a distorted concept of responsibility, it is productive to consider the limits of responsibility within a family setting, especially as it relates to parenting.

God is no less of a god because his children make wrong choices. God's value, his character, and his love are not changed by any external factor. The gift of agency and accountability is for our eternal progression, not to manage the choices of others. We are children of God, and we should emulate our Heavenly Parents in shepherding the children with which we have been blessed.

Doctrine and Covenants 58:26 further teaches the boundaries of being a more holy parent: "For behold, it is not meet that I should command in all things; for he that is compelled in all things, the same is a slothful and not a wise servant; wherefore he receiveth no reward." Compelled obedience is not fit for a disciple of Christ; therefore, it is not appropriate in parenting. If you are a parent and you feel the urge to compel your children, this is a double sign that proper teaching of correct principles is not in place. Perhaps the responsibility to "govern themselves" has not properly been extended or accepted. This codependent parenting model will burn out parents and place a wall to the progress of children.

True gospel principles, when taught in love and with the spirit of promise, are sufficient to motivate our best desires towards fulfilling our greatest potential. Parents don't need to repackage the gospel for the home. If the gospel of Jesus Christ is sufficient to exalt the world, it is sufficient to tutor children to become honorable disciples. Learn the gospel, and teach it in love and faith. Trust in the Lord that what he has set as the plan of salvation for the world also has power to improve families. The Family Proclamation teaches this very principle: "Happiness in family life is most likely to be achieved when founded upon the teachings of the Lord Jesus Christ. Successful marriages and families are established and maintained on principles of faith, prayer, repentance, forgiveness, respect, love, compassion, work, and wholesome recreational activities."

Remember to forgive our children and to forgive ourselves. Holding on to the mistakes of the past can push an individual towards codependency. Mistakes are part of the mortal experience, and part of how we learn. We should not fear mistakes when they are made by ourselves or others. We should not fear forgiving others or seeking forgiveness when we have made mistakes. Well-intentioned individuals will fall short from time to time, and it is important to avoid becoming weakened and depressed by those occurrences.

This is a difficult, if not painful, realization to come to. For the codependent parent, there may even be a nagging and anxiety-based response that has set up shop in your brain simply by reading this section. These intense feelings may cause you to enact some regimen of apologies or steps to fix the sins of the past immediately. Others may have started a steady stream of justifications for their behavior that blame others for your behaviors. The compulsion to use "if _____ then ____" statements to explain away the past may feel like a natural response. For those feeling this tension, take a deep breath. Maybe take a moment to write down your thoughts and your feelings. Write about the areas where you may have behaved codependently towards a child. Whatever you do, don't write a press release where you only tell yourself the parts you want to see. Don't spin your mortal experience; learn from it. Be honest, and let the pains you feel sort of sit there for a minute. The more it hurts, the less likely you are to act in a way that continues the hurt in the future. Breathe through the emotions of coming to the realization of your past actions as mistakes. It is possible to start today with an apology for past mistakes combined with the genuine but not anxiety-filled commitment to be better. That's repentance.

IF YOU RECOGNIZE CODEPENDENT TENDENCIES IN
YOURSELF, HOW DO THEY SHOW UP IN YOUR
PARENTING? HOW MUCH DO YOU WANT TO RESCUE
YOUR YOUNG ADULT CHILDREN FROM THE CHOICES
THEY MAKE? HOW MUCH UNSOLICITED ADVICE DO
YOU GIVE? HOW DO YOU DECIDE WHEN TO LET AN
ADULT CHILD STRUGGLE THROUGH THEIR OWN
CONSEQUENCES?

Social Media

Social media is a powerful internet-based tool used to facilitate easy communication and transmission of content among like-minded individuals, friends, family, or even celebrities and public figures for which there is no pre-existing relationship. With a few words, individuals are given the power to share their thoughts with anyone who will listen. Political positions are announced, favorite restaurants are showcased, and pictures and videos are shared with the ease of a click on a keyboard or mouse. Media that creates revenues for social media platforms in the amounts of billions of dollars is transmitted seemingly without discernment or discipline.

Regardless of the intent of its creation, social media has become a necessary part of society for many people. The way that people process information from social media has shifted to a platform where rapid fire data seems to elicit a rapid fire and consistent response. The world up to this point has survived without social media, yet many today, an overwhelming number of users it would seem, have created a pattern of behaviors where sharing the day's events and waiting for external gratification has become commonplace. Facebook, Twitter, Snapchat, and other platforms are financially motivated by keeping users connected; the more connected people are, the more effective these products become.

Social media use can be considered codependent when one compulsively shares pictures, videos, and commentary, and when this compulsive and unmanageable behavior seems to form a person's identity and emotions. If an individual is unable to stop the practice of continuously engaging in social media, they are likely either addicted themselves or possibly codependent as they are basing their individual worth and value on the easily facilitated opinions of others through social media. Some cannot eat a meal without first checking in to the restaurant on social media, taking a picture of their food, and waiting for people to comment on their post while waiting for their food to arrive.

Many Facebook users, Twitter followers, and Snapchat users wake up and spend their first 20-50 minutes on their mobile devices seeing "what's happening." Users cannot begin the day without offering comments or "likes" on scores of status updates, news pieces, blog posts, or their favorite cat video. In many ways, social media has become the economic force of the world, helping to drive public opinion on products, movies, events, and many other product categories.

According to an article in *Business Insider,* Facebook users average 40-50 minutes (or more) on Facebook (and related messaging apps) a day. One can assume, as with all averages, some will not spend any time on Facebook but still have an account. This implies that the real average time on Facebook for active users is likely well over an hour a day. With the latest figures stating that there are 1.71 billion active users (1.57 billion mobile users alone) on Facebook every day, that means that about 1.71 billion hours of otherwise productive time is spent performing the 4.5 billion "likes" and "shares" instead.

To draw back to the key points of codependency, we can see that many social media users fit the category of codependency. "Codependent relationships are a type of dysfunctional helping relationship where one person supports or enables another person's poor mental health, immaturity, irresponsibility, or under-achievement."

While some can affix spikes in certain codependent-like activities on Facebook to political seasons or other matters of social concern, social media users in general seem to feel an undeniable need to save everyone they can from the evils they perceive taking place. From campaigning against a bad vote for "the other person" to virtue signaling, social media has produced more supposed "victims" to more issues and consequently brought more pressure to social causes than any other platform in human history. One's daily Facebook feed is filled with story after story of victim after victim. Each day people are bombarded by the view of a world that appears to be sick and in desperate need of humanity and worldwide saving.

These stories are shared because it taps into our human nature to want to remove or alleviate suffering, and this can be a good thing. However, these interactions can become crusades where individuals are made to feel responsible for acts and decisions in which they had no part. There is an ever-changing standard of acceptable moral behavior driven by social acceptance over eternal principle. Those who don't comply with these changing standards can expect to be ridiculed or even "unfriended"–the social media equivalent of being banished or a cessation of an in-person relationships. There are so many ways in which individuals on social media feel or develop the compulsion to do something, not out of charity or pure love, but because "there is so much evil in the world, and unless you do something about it you are a bad person." That is not to say people shouldn't be kind, but posting about it could, in fact, be making the problem worse. The constant barrage of evils that we should all be aware of, and aren't likely doing enough to fix, can fuel the fire of codependency.

While some might categorize Facebook as something that people are addicted to, and there is some merit to that argument, a growing number of behaviors show that social media displays the world in such contextually void arguments that we find ourselves debating and discussing things that will largely do very little to improve the world—it can only make us feel guilty for not "liking" the right thing. With every political post the user is saying, "Here is a social ill or political issue. Now, you fix it, you respond to it, you need to feel my emotions about this _____ (fill in the blank)."

When individuals become codependent, their lives become unmanageable and out of control, largely because they feel that there are so many people that need saving that they become bogged down and even shut down emotionally because they can no longer sustain the pain that comes from the constant empathy or effort needed to fix the ills they see. They quickly feel down on themselves for not doing all that the world seems to demand of them.

In social media, repeated victimization either creates codependency with some cause or the opinions of others or fosters codependency in how we react to the cries for help and attention. In any case, social media networks function exclusively on the basis that people have a habit of coming back to the site, over and over again, or their users will be lost without it. Social media platforms are designed to organize an argument and offer notifications and reminders of the "conversation" so that we can return to it again and again. People base their self-worth on the number of likes their status updates receive and the number of people who reach out to alleviate their plights.

Consider for a moment the nature of social media itself. If using social media weren't about getting attention or feeding off the responses of others, we would just write our thoughts and opinions down in a journal or something private. The intent and power of a social media platform is by its nature to make these things known publicly, and not in some passive way but in a way where people "like" and comment on these things. Our opinions tend to have more or less value in our own minds based on how many people react to what we have said. Some use the apps and the website to such a habitual degree that few hours pass in the day when they aren't somehow connected to the social media world. All of this combined is a pattern of behavior that is mentally and emotionally unsustainable. Social media interaction almost programs the world to be codependent.

Read again this definition of codependency: "A codependent is someone who cannot function from their innate self and whose thinking and behavior is instead organized around another person, or even a process, or substance." Is social media not organized around other people or processes of communication and interaction? Do people get a chemical reaction, a psychological reaction to the things that people post on Facebook? Of course. That is how it is designed. That is why we can "Like," "Heart or Love," "Be Sad," or other emojis to respond to what people post. We can share, we can retweet—we are being programmed to respond to anything and everything in lightning fast ways and in the growing convenience of mobile devices.

It is due to this prevalence that social media users would do well to see just how long they can go without participating in social media, including what they might consider to be a passive experience. Experiment on the idea that individuals seem completely different when you meet them in real life than they are on social media. Are they the same people? Do they seem to behave differently when online? If so, why? Is it because they are filling an emotional need that they cannot seem to fill on their own? A great many of the growing trends in social media decorum seem driven by the underlying principles that define codependency.

On some level this notion will likely create some backlash among those who feel that this assessment of social media is painted with too broad a brush. Admittedly, it is one of the less discussed or proven applications of codependency. We have no objection to keeping this issue in the realm of theory as opposed to documentary history. However, considering the strong rise in "victimization" as the common theme in the discourse of most outcries on social media, it is not that far a leap to see social media's reinforcing influence on codependent victimization.

This is one area where individuals feel prompted to advertise their faith crisis (please see "Faith Crisis" in this chapter for more). For some, it isn't enough to experience a faith crisis in patience, trust, or isolation. Faith crisis becomes part of their external persona and identity. Social media outlets can be a convenient way to broadcast their "need" for help, to be saved from their pain, or to find external validation that will help them "feel better." While some do this as a cry for help, others do it as a method of deferring ownership of their problems to other people. One's faith is their own responsibility. No amount of putting out a cry for help on social media will change that accountability.

Social media is filled with emotional litter. This can contribute to a sense that the world is a filthy, messy, garbage-filled existence. Seeing this growing pile of other people's problems causes many to develop a codependent response. After all, who is going to clean up the mess if it isn't them? Some people will use their "influence" on social media to dump their emotional garbage all over the place, and then claim anyone who doesn't pick it up is immoral. This pattern of behavior has become so popular that hundreds of millions have subscribed to these voices and "feed" off this toxic waste to the detriment of their otherwise charitable soul.

WHEN YOU'RE SCROLLING SOCIAL MEDIA, IS PART OF YOUR BRAIN MONITORING WHAT CERTAIN PEOPLE POST SO THAT YOU CAN SEE HOW TO "FIX" THEM? WHEN SOMEONE DOES AN EMOTIONAL PLEA ON SOCIAL MEDIA FOR ATTENTION, DO YOU FEEL LIKE YOU MUST RESPOND? DO YOU SEE YOURSELF AS A HEARTLESS PERSON IF YOU DON'T? DO YOU FEEL LIKE YOU MUST BE ABSOLUTELY UP-TO-DATE ON CERTAIN PEOPLE'S SOCIAL MEDIA SO THAT YOU CAN HELP THEM MANAGE THEIR UNMANAGEABLE LIVES?

Unmet Needs

By now you have probably come to understand that codependent behavior is driven by unmet needs. And if anything you have read resonates with you—feelings of shame, embarrassment, guilt, or worse—it may be helpful to consider what unmet needs you have developed. No one likes to think of themselves as having unmet needs, and we certainly don't like to think of ourselves as hurting others because of them. But if a problem can be recognized, it likely can be fixed.

The goal of healing codependency is not for you to feel more isolated or to have less access to love and relationships. It's so that you can have *more* of those things. Listen to the words of the apostle Peter:

> "If then, through the submission to the truth, your souls have been made pure so as to engender in you an unfeigned love, let the love you bear one another be one that comes from the heart and is ever fervent" (1 Peter 1:22).

Our divine design predisposes us to thrive in healthy relationships. In other words, we were made for relationships. Heavenly Father did not create us to live in isolation but to live in families and groups. Zion society mirrors that of a celestial glory. But these associations are empowering and exalting, not parasitic. The places where codependency has snuck in and made charity a challenge can be rooted out through "submission to the truth," as Peter says. For diagnosing codependency, submitting to the truth must start with a humble honesty that asks, "Is this me? Am I the one who must heal?"

Part of the reason why healing from codependency is difficult is that the unmet needs have to be faced. Those unmet needs might represent hurts that you have been running from for a lifetime. If codependency has been the "medication" that dulls your pain, disengaging codependency will likely bring that pain to the surface. We can take encouragement from the psalmist when he says:

> I sought the LORD, and he heard me, and delivered me from all my fears. We looked unto him, and were lightened: and our faces were not ashamed. The poor man cried, and the LORD heard him, and saved him out of all his troubles.[71]

In order to recover from codependency you are going to need the strength and love of Heavenly Father—and you may also need the spiritual direction of your bishop, the wisdom of a good therapist, the community of brothers and sisters available to you in the Church, and wholesome distractions to help you get through the tough times. But progressing in healing IS possible.

WHILE READING THROUGH THIS BOOK DO YOU
RECOGNIZE ANY WAYS IN WHICH YOU ARE TRYING
TO FILL YOUR OWN NEEDS BY FIXING OTHERS? DO
YOU FEAR THAT IF YOU STOP BEING CODEPENDENT
(OR FIXING THINGS FOR SOMEONE) THEY WILL EXIT
YOUR LIFE? DO YOU FEEL READY TO DO THE WORK
TO MEET YOUR OWN UNMET NEEDS?

Chapter 6 - Conclusion

"Therefore if any man be in Christ, he is a new
creature: old things are passed away; behold,
all things are become new."

2 Corinthians 5:17

———— ♦ ————

To answer the question that I am sure many reading this volume are asking: No, we were not paid by the number of times we wrote the word *codependency* or *codependent*. If there was a recognized compulsive disorder for repetitive word use in writing, we would need to get that checked. While "that word" has likely appeared on every page, it is for good reason. However, for those who are feeling burdened by the repetition of that word, we empathize with your pain.

We also recognize the potential irony of a couple of people with a history of codependency writing a book that we hope will "help" people. Some may even wonder if this whole book isn't just one big codependent attempt to "fix" people. The thought has crossed our minds. But, in the event that is true, then it is not your responsibility to fix, now is it! (See how that works?)

Joking aside, this is a serious enough subject, and of a large enough scope that we hope this text can help you to see the world in a more productive way. When sifting through the daily feed of your social media, or listening to the 24/7 news cycle, we hope you are less compelled towards un-Christlike behaviors or the anxiety-ridden compulsion to save the world. This isn't to say the world doesn't need some help. But we need to recognize who the real Savior is. Just remember, recovery is challenging, but it is also empowering.

Discipleship is a rewarding and exalting endeavor. However, "putting off the natural man"[72] is a challenging enough endeavor without adding to it. Many carry burdens through this life and don't know how to find reprieve. If codependency is on the list of burdens you carry—meaning you are carrying more than you can or should carry—we hope to have provided you some answers that can lead to solutions. If you find yourself among those who see the world "in commotion" and "men's hearts [are failing] them,"[73] and if you feel an anxiety-ridden urge to "fix it all," we invite you to strongly consider what we have shared. May grace attend you on your path to greater peace and a more healthy relationship with yourself, with others, with the Church, and with God.

CODEPENDENT DISCIPLESHIP

by Nick Galieti & Jennifer Roach MDiv, MA, LMHC, CDP

Endnotes

1. Doctrine and Covenants 88:91
2. Fosdick, Harry Emerson Twelve Tests of Character [1923], 87-88).
3. Mosiah 18:8-9
4. Obadiah 1:21
5. Kimball, Spencer W. Teachings of Presidents of the Church: Spencer W. Kimball [2006], 82
6. These approaches will be discussed in further detail in Chapter 4.
7. Some may call this the "WebMD syndrome." Individuals can read symptoms on the Internet and become convinced that they have the disease they are reading about. Symptoms don't always tell the whole story.
8. The DSM or Diagnostic and Statistical Manual of Mental Disorders is published by the American Psychiatric Association and is the most widely used source for the classification of mental disorders in the United States. In some ways it can be considered for the Mental Health Professionals what the Holy Bible is to Christians.
9. An illicit substance abuse disorder is a bit clearer as one can entirely eliminate consuming these if they want to, whereas food is a necessary part of human existence.
10. Smyer, Ingrid Frances Relationship Within p. 202
11. For more information on this definition: Anderson, S.C. (1994). "A critical analysis of the concept of codependency." Social Work. 39 (6): 677–685.
12. See Chapter 4 - Treatments for Trauma-based Codependency
13. Schnarch, David, Intimacy & Desire: Awaken the passion in your relationship
14. See Chapter 5 - Unmet Needs
15. This book is discussed in further detail in Chapter 4.
16. Holland, David F. "Latter-day Saints and the Problem of Pain," Maxwell Lecture, BYU October 29, 2016
17. LDS Perspectives Podcast Interview with David F. Holland, Episode

34, May 3, 2017

18. Doctrine and Covenants 88:118

19. Baker, LeGrand L. "Free agency and Truth" Retrieved on May 6, 2020 http://www.legrandlbaker.org/2014/02/12/1-nephi-39-15-legrand-baker-free-agency-and-truth/

20. Doctrine and Covenants 82:3

21. Doctrine and Covenants 121:36-37; emphasis added

22. Lewis, C.S., God in the Dock: Essays on Theology (Making of Modern Theology)

23. See Chapter 5, Missionary Service

24. The use of orthopathy in this context is not relating to the medical term, but rather to the more religious or spiritual connotation.

25. Doctrine and Covenants 11:21

26. Matthew 5:14

27. Oaks, Dallin H. "Our Strengths Can Become Our Downfall." From an address given at a Brigham Young University eighteen-stake fireside on 7 June 1992 in Provo, Utah

28. Mosiah 3:19

29. See Chapter 5 - Parenting and Transitioning Children into Adulthood

30. Retrieved from https://www.churchofjesuschrist.org/study/ensign/2019/09/young-adults/understanding-scrupulosity-religious-ocd?lang=eng on May 27, 2020. McClendon, Debra Theobald, PhD - Understanding Scrupulosity (Religious OCD)

31. Retrieved from https://www.churchofjesuschrist.org/study/ensign/2019/09/young-adults/understanding-scrupulosity-religious-ocd?lang=eng on May 27, 2020. McClendon, Debra Theobald, PhD - Understanding Scrupulosity (Religious OCD)

32. Alma 5:14-15

33. Mosiah 4:27

34. Matthew 10:39

35. Maxwell, Neal A. "Wisdom and Order" June 1994 Ensign

36. Mosiah 18:8

37. Holland, Jeffrey R. "Be Ye Therefore Perfect—Eventually." October 2017 General Conference

38. Ibid.

39. Matthew 7:3

40. Beattie, Meoldy Codependent No More: How to Stop Controlling Others and Start Caring for Yourself p. 38

41. Back Cover synopsis of "Loving What Is" published by Three Rivers Press 2002.

42. Katie, Byron "Loving What Is" p.3-4 2002 paperback version.

43. Retrieved from https://www.psychologytoday.com/us/therapy-types/dialectical-behavior-therapy

44. Doctrine and Covenants 93:24

45. Visit https://addictionrecovery.churchofjesuschrist.org/spouses-and-families for more information or search "Spouse and Family Support Guide" on the Church's addiction recovery website.

46. Cambridge Dictionary (online). Retrieved from website on Feb 17, 2021. https://dictionary.cambridge.org/us/dictionary/english/cancel-culture

47. Doctrine and Covenants 64:8-11

48. 2 Nephi 28:30, Isaiah 28:13, Doctrine and Covenants 98:12

49. Alma 12:24

50. Uchtdorf, Dieter F., "Perfect Love Chaseth Out Fear," April 2017 General Conference

51. 1 Corinthians 13:8

52. Holland, Jeffrey R. "Live a Broken Vessel," 2013 October General Conference

53. Luke 10:38-42

54. McLellan, Jeffrey S. "Thy Troubles to Bless," July 10, 2018 BYU Devotional

55. See "Social Media" section in this chapter

56. "The Family: A Proclamation to the World," The First Presidency and Council of the Twelve Apostles of The Church of Jesus Christ of Latter-day Saints

57. Retrived from the Guide to the Scriptures, https://www.churchofjesuschrist.org/study/scriptures/gs/consecrate-law-of-consecration?lang=eng June 4, 2020

58. Mosiah 4:27

59. "Letterbook 1," p. 46, The Joseph Smith Papers, accessed June 3, 2020, https://www.josephsmithpapers.org/paper-summary/letterbook-1/58; original spelling and punctuation preserved.

60. Moroni 9:6

61. Jacob 1:19

62. Doctrine and Covenants 107:99-100

63. "Hazy" performed by Rosi Golan, song written by Iain Denis Archer, Rosi Golan, Richard Emanuel Lobb

64. "Baby Love" performed by The Supremes, written by Brian Holland, Lamont Dozier, and Eddie Holland

65. "When Something Is Wrong with My Baby" Written by: Isaac Hayes, David Porter

66. Other song examples include (but are not limited to): "I Hate Myself For Loving You" - Joan Jett and the Blackhearts; "Right Here" by Staind; "Can't Smile Without You" by Barry Manilow--to name a few.

67. Doctrine and Covenants 68:25

68. Doctrine and Covenants 64:9-11

69. Baker, LeGrand L. "Joseph and Moroni: 7 The 7 Principles Moroni Taught Joseph Smith p. 43-44

70. Messages of the First Presidency, comp. James R. Clark, 6 vols., Salt Lake City: Bookcraft, 1965–75, 3:54.

71. Psalm 34:4-6

72. Mosiah 3:19

73. Doctrine and Covenants 88:91 (adjusted text for grammatical consistency)

Please join us on Facebook for our Codependent Discussion Group, as well as regular content to help and inspire those struggling with this issue.

https://www.facebook.com/CodependentDiscipleship

Made in the USA
Middletown, DE
18 April 2022

64342662R00151